# STATE
## *of* PLAY

**ALSO BY BILL RIPKEN:**

*Coaching Youth Baseball The Ripken Way*
(with Cal Ripken Jr.)

*Play Baseball The Ripken Way*
(with Cal Ripken Jr.)

# BILL RIPKEN

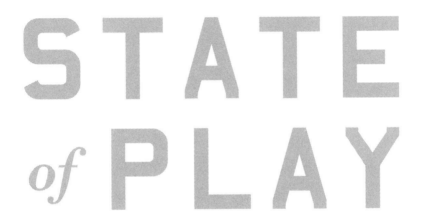

# STATE *of* PLAY

## THE OLD SCHOOL GUIDE TO
### *NEW SCHOOL BASEBALL*

DIVERSION
BOOKS

For more information, email info@diversionbooks.com

Diversion Books
A division of Diversion Publishing Corp.
443 Park Avenue South, suite 1004
New York, NY 10016
www.diversionbooks.com

Book design by Aubrey Khan, Neuwirth & Associates

First Diversion Books edition, February 2020
Hardcover ISBN: 978-1-63576-659-2
eBook ISBN: 978-1-63576-660-8

Printed in The United States of America

1  3  5  7  9  10  8  6  4  2

Library of Congress cataloging-in-publication data is available on file.

*For my wife, Candace, and my kids, Miranda, Anna, Reese, and Jack. Everything I have become is because of you guys.*

# CONTENTS

Foreword by Ken Rosenthal                                        xi

Introduction                                                     xv

I   Cal Ripken Sr.                                     1

2   The Ripken Way                                      11

3   Pitch Framing                                       21

4   Launch Angle                                        29

5   Spin Rate                                           39

6   Pitching Wins                                       47

7   Tunneling                                           55

8   Batting Average Versus On-Base Percentage           61

9   Wins Above Replacement (WAR)                        67

10   Defensive Runs Saved (DRS)                         79

11   Overshifts and Defensive Positioning              87

12   Errors                                             101

13   Automated Strike Zone and Ball-Strike Umpires     109

14   Runs Batted In (RBI)                               117

15   On-Base Plus Slugging (OPS)                        121

16   The Designated Hitter                              127

17   The Game Being Played                              135

18   The Control Group                                  141

19   Positional Versatility, Bench Players, and Platooning  147

20   Unwritten Rules                                    153

21   Run Differential                                   159

22   Lineup Construction                                163

# CONTENTS

**23**  Weather and Baseball                 177

**24**  Phrases of the Game                  181

**25**  The Future                           189


Acknowledgments                             195

About the Author                            197

Photo Credits                               199

Index                                       201

# STATE
*of* PLAY

I don't recall exactly when the conversation took place—it was fifteen years ago, maybe more. At the time, many in baseball were dismissive of advanced statistical analysis. And while the analysts clearly had something to offer, their tone was often condescending and occasionally nasty, turning off many of us who otherwise were open to their ideas.

Around that time I became friendly with an analyst who was much more measured than many of his peers were. One day I asked him, "Why are so many in the sabermetric community so hostile to those who do not embrace their arguments?" I will never forget his response: "Because when no one will listen, you have to shout to be heard."

All these years later, baseball's cultural war continues; only the power dynamic has reversed. Every team relies heavily on data, employing numerous analysts who influence both on- and off-field decisions. And now it's members of what Bill Ripken calls the "old school"—scouts, coaches, and executives with a more traditional bent—who struggle to be heard.

Until now, that is.

If you know Bill, you know he is a proud member of the old school. You know he is bursting with baseball knowledge. And you know he is not one to use his inside voice when he wants to deliver a powerful message.

Bill is a product of one of the game's great baseball families, a former major league infielder who is now an Emmy Award–

winning studio analyst for MLB Network. His job at the network keeps him current with the game's trends, but it doesn't mean he accepts them as gospel. In this book, he lays out his objections to a number of new practices. And as someone who talks daily with people in both camps, I can assure you he is not speaking only for himself.

I first met Bill in 1987, his rookie year with the Orioles and my first year as a baseball writer for the *Baltimore (Evening) Sun*. We didn't agree on everything when I covered him, and we don't agree on everything now. But as the son of Cal Ripken Sr., who spent thirty-six years in the Orioles' organization as a player, coach, and manager, Bill grew up in the game and was good enough to play it at the highest level. His baseball IQ is such that many in the sport believe he would make a great major league coach. Yet too often today, baseball people like him are treated as if they have nothing to offer, despite their lifetime of experience in the game.

Virtually every team claims that it blends the old and new ways of thinking, using both subjective and objective information, valuing input from traditional scouts along with statistical analysts. With some clubs, those assertions ring true. With others, they're lip service. Some in the new school—both members of the media and members of front offices—simply are unwilling to explore the ideas Bill presents, treating them almost as threatening.

In this book, Bill writes, among other things, about all of the variables that might affect a player's defensive rating. About why the path to a called strike is more nuanced than pitch-framing statistics indicate. About how a player such as Bill's older brother, Cal Jr., was his own information bank, relying on his own wits to position himself instinctively—and effectively—without the need for data-driven overshifting.

Bill doesn't have all the answers. No one in baseball does. But he is taking the same approach the new school analysts did as they rose to prominence, posing questions that challenge the game's accepted doctrines. Only now, the accepted doctrines are the ones espoused by the new school, and some members of that school are as resistant to different ideas as the traditionalists once were.

A form of baseball détente is necessary. The new schoolers need to listen to those who understand what it is like to play the game. The old schoolers need to accept that baseball has evolved. As I wrote recently for *The Athletic*, "The sport isn't going back. It *shouldn't* go back. But the flexibility in thought the new school demanded—the relentless quest for knowledge that is the very basis of sabermetrics—should work both ways."

That's all Bill is asking. Seems pretty reasonable to me.

—Ken Rosenthal
MLB Network analyst
September 2019

The way we talk about baseball has changed, but the game and the reasons for a player's or team's success really haven't changed all that much over the years. Baseball is still baseball and what has been done and worked for years is still being done and working in the game today. That's old school. Those claiming that the game is completely different now are just making noise. Some things are different, sure, but they may not be as good as they once were. Take strikeouts. The rise of strikeouts to record levels over the past few years reflects a shift toward a philosophy in which "an out is an out." Productive outs, battling with two strikes, and putting the ball in play have always been old school. And if the new and improved is neither new nor improved, we need to take a closer look.

This book isn't about what happens in any one season. These are my honest observations of what I've seen in the game, both past and present, and what I believe will happen in the game's future. If my theories and observations are sound as I continue to use baseball common sense as my guide, they will still ring true twenty years from now, or more.

I've been in this game my entire life and I still love it. That's why I'm writing this book. My coaching experience, combined with what I learned playing the game and in my work for MLB Network has cemented my views on how the game is and should be played. In the twenty-plus years that I have spent coaching young players and teaching youth coaches as part of Ripken

Baseball, I've learned that the most complex situations are usually the product of simple things. A 6-4-3 double play at any level is a catch-throw-catch-throw-catch. Baseball isn't rocket science. It's a game that needs some thought, but not overthinking. Pitch the ball, catch the ball, and hit the ball better than the other team does and you win. Give me a starting pitcher who hands me a lead after seven innings and I like my chances in this game and the next one. Give me four infielders with average range and good

Had a good swing here while Sr. looked on from the third base coach's box.

hands who want to play 155-plus games a year, and I'll take my chances with them as well. Give me two guys who are beasts in the batter's box so I can hit them third and fourth in my lineup, and I'll figure the rest out. If that sounds like an oversimplification, so be it. With so many trying to complicate the game today, fighting fire with fire makes sense to me.

I've never taken on a project like this one before. I've learned I'm not a novelist, but I know I have something to say. There's just so much being introduced or forced into the game today that a handbook that can address some of these new things in an easy-to-understand way is needed. Watching the game still looks pretty much the same, but listening to what is said during the game is a whole other animal. If you hear a term during a game that doesn't quite register with you, I hope this book can help.

New school baseball minds use information and numbers to reach their conclusions, but intelligent baseball people have been using information and numbers for decades. Those people are a large part of how I define the "old school." The old school baseball guy has always used information and numbers to help create a plan for success. He's been around for a long time. Old school doesn't mean outdated or obsolete, it means battle-tested. Thirty, forty, and fifty years ago, box scores, scouting reports, and prior matchups were all used to come up with game plans for any given day. Any time valuable information presented itself, it was processed and used accordingly. This was across the board, whether evaluating a possible trade, a free agent on the open market, the June draft, bringing up a player from the minor leagues, the organization of spring training, or simply getting ready for game day.

The old school baseball guy will also use his eyes as the game unfolds, and if his eyes see something that contradicts certain numbers, he might go with what he sees. The old school baseball guy wrestles with himself over the results of decisions he made during the course of a game. He understands that the game is built on results, that a broken bat hit is always better than a line drive out. The new school baseball guy trusts his numbers and the formulas more than he trusts his eyes.

If a starting pitcher has had a rough time going through a line up a third time, he may find himself being new schooled out of the game in the sixth inning no matter how he is pitching that day. Let's say in this particular case, the starter being removed has a three-to-one lead and gets hooked. The bullpen happens to give up the goods and the team goes on to lose. If an old school guy made the pitching decision, he would kick himself for not trusting his eyes and instead going by the book. But the new school guy lives and dies by the numbers.

I like numbers as much as the next guy, but the numbers are not the game. Matchup statistics have been used in this game for a long time by old school and new school guys alike, but there's a difference in the way we use them. Old school guys will use them while watching the game unfold to maybe ride a hot hand, whereas I believe new school guys are more likely to stick with their spreadsheets and play the percentages. I understand the percentage approach to a degree, but the game has too many variables to allow for a one-size-fits-all approach. While players' statistics and their past performances present interesting matchup scenarios, so does the most current action from the game at hand. The game being played should be a huge factor in any baseball manager's decision-making process, along with the numbers, and old school managers understand that.

Of course there was less information back in the day, and it was limited in how it was distributed. But make no mistake about it: Whatever information was worthy of being used was used. There's this stereotype of the hardcore, crusty, no-nonsense baseball guy that he just throws the bats and balls out onto the field and with no plan whatsoever and says, "Go get 'em." That's not the case and it never was.

Over the past few years there has been an overwhelming amount of discussion about how much the game has changed. New school baseball guys are now in charge, and things are being done and viewed in a way that's drastically different than they were in the past. There is a wide range within this new school, from "all-in hardcore" believers to those who simply "see a place for this," and everything in between. The members of this new school movement have certainly infiltrated major league front offices, baseball operations departments, player development, and scouting. Some of their thinking has trickled down to the field, where new school–leaning managers ply their trade. But I believe there are some concepts being introduced and implemented into this game that completely go against baseball common sense. I also believe that some of these things will soften or disappear entirely over time as we see that one-plus-one on paper doesn't always equal two on the baseball field.

Hiring younger presidents of baseball operations and general managers is the in-vogue move for major league clubs these days. Lesser paid, less experienced managers in some teams' dugouts are replacing the higher paid, more experienced managers of the past. This is telling me that the manager of today's game doesn't have as much responsibility or power as managers had in years past. I'm not discounting today's managers' role in a team's success or failure; I'm just saying that the definition of what, specifically, they are in charge of has changed. And I believe that it is less than what it used to be. I do believe that there are some young front offices and managers who collaborate, get along well, and have success. The Atlanta Braves and Tampa Bay Rays are prime examples. These pairings have a respect for what one another bring to the table. This isn't a new dynamic in baseball; the

Atlanta Braves' John Schuerholz and Bobby Cox had a pretty good run together back in the day, winning fourteen consecutive division titles and a World Series in 1995. We also witnessed a bit of a new school-old school hybrid as we watched the 2018 Red Sox win a World Series with one of the most experienced front-office leaders in Dave Dombrowski working with a first-year manager in Alex Cora. Let's also point out that in 1998, when a thirty-one-year-old first-year general manager Brian Cashman paired up with heavily-experienced manager Joe Torre, the Yankees won their first of three straight World Series.

I have no issue with the new school being directly involved in baseball. I believe it brings a little bit of a different perspective to the game and a whole lot of passion. This group brings ideas to the table that provoke conversation with the baseball people, assuming they keep them. Some of these ideas and thoughts aren't exactly brand new; they've been kicked around for years. But while it never hurts to revisit an idea, it's likely that if it didn't work the first time, it probably won't work the second time around either. In fairness, the majority of the new school group aren't dictator types who tell the baseball people in their organization that it's their way or the highway. There are some in this group, however, who do have way too much involvement in the day-to-day operations of their club. That said, I feel that the better teams of today strike a balance between the new and the old. Most of the new school front offices still understand that the guys in the clubhouse who play the game—under some good, old-fashioned baseball coaching—*are* the game, and that the successes to be had happen on the field. I'm also sure that a few of the hardcore, new school front offices are a little bit too smart for their own good. If any team does push the new too far, it will show and then, over time, they will return to a more traditional baseball setup. This has happened with a few ball clubs in the last couple of years and it will happen in the years to come, too, as some of the things being done today will reveal themselves to be flawed.

The fact that many in the new school have not been directly involved in the game is far more alarming to me. This group is becoming more and more responsible for spreading misleading information about how much the game has changed and how much of an impact their new school methods have had on the game. They will try to take credit for a team's or player's success. This is puzzling to me, as this group has nothing to do with the actual game. Saying something over and over again doesn't make it true. Providing answers by using catchy phrases without any explanation or understanding of what really goes on in the game doesn't do it for me. If information analysis is the key to this new school group's methodology, then having all the information before making definitive blanket statements should be a standard practice. Making blanket statements based off one or two catch-phrases or coming to absolute resolutions based on something weighted, created, or adjusted doesn't do it for me either.

Newly established statistics are running wild through the game's landscape with seemingly no governing body to monitor them. Some of these new statistics are being rushed to market only to quickly lose their meaning when applied to real baseball common sense. Some of these stats have already become extinct over the past few years to a degree, as some members of the new school aren't using them anymore. There is even infighting within subfactions of the new school regarding which stats and numbers are valid. I don't believe the organizations themselves rush the numbers, though. They all keep their own numbers, and I believe that those numbers might be quite different from the numbers that reach the public. These numbers are theirs and theirs alone.

Has the game changed? Many in the new school will tell you yes. In fact they will stand on their soapbox with a megaphone and tell you that most everything in the game that is working well is because of their brand-spanking-new innovations. But baseball has always had its trends, some of a cyclical nature—fading away only to come back into play while others fade away and never return.

The Houston Astros are at the forefront of the new school revolution and have done a great job of putting themselves in a position to be World Series contenders year after year. It has been said that the 2017 World Series champions were smarter, doing things differently than all the other organizations, and that's what allowed them to win it all. Are they smart? And do they do some things differently? Yes, I believe they are. And yes, I believe they do. But I also believe that the 2017 Astros were built in a similar way to almost any other World Series champion in recent memory.

The 2017 Houston Astros reached and won the World Series with a core of Carlos Correa, George Springer, José Altuve, Alex Bregman, and Dallas Keuchel. That homegrown core could have been as good as any other team's homegrown core over the past twenty-five seasons. They were also able to add front-line starter Justin Verlander at the trading deadline in exchange for three prospects, a trade that was vital to their winning the championship. That proving successful, they packaged four more prospects in a trade for ace Gerrit Cole the following January. In 2019 the Astros lost Keuchel to free agency, but they still had Verlander and Cole to build a rotation around. Being able to add pitchers of Verlander's and Cole's quality without giving up established major league talent is a testament to the strength of the Astros minor league system. Instead of adding farm-grown pitchers to their core position players, they traded prospects to gain established starting pitchers. This held true once again as the Astros pulled off another trade deadline gem by acquiring Zack Greinke from the Arizona Diamondbacks for four minor league players.

Trading eleven possible future big league players for your top three starting pitchers seems like an old school approach to me.

Think about the teams in Wild Card era (since 1995) that have gone to multiple World Series, each having at least two home-grown core position players, one homegrown starting pitcher, and one homegrown reliever.

## NOTABLE TEAMS TO MAKE MULTIPLE WORLD SERIES APPEARANCES SINCE 1995

### Atlanta Braves: 1995–1996, 1999
- Position players: Chipper Jones, David Justice (1995), Ryan Klesko, Javy Lopez, Andruw Jones
- Starting pitchers: Tom Glavine, Steve Avery (1995-1996), Kevin Millwood (1999)
- Relief pitcher: Mark Wohlers (1995-1996), John Rocker (1999)

### Cleveland Indians: 1995, 1997
- Position players: Manny Ramirez, Jim Thome, Albert Belle (1995)
- Starting pitchers: Charles Nagy, Jaret Wright (1997), Chad Ogea
- Relief pitcher: Julián Tavárez

### New York Yankees: 1996, 1998–2001, 2003, 2009
- Position players: Bernie Williams (1996, 1998-2001, 2003), Derek Jeter, Jorge Posada
- Starting pitcher: Andy Pettitte
- Relief pitcher: Mariano Rivera

• • •

### Boston Red Sox: 2007, 2013, 2018

- Position players: Dustin Pedroia, Jacoby Ellsbury (2007), Xander Bogaerts (2013, 2018), Mookie Betts, Andrew Benintendi, Jackie Bradley Jr.
- Starting pitcher: Jon Lester (2007, 2013)
- Relief pitcher: Jonathan Papelbon (2007)

### San Francisco Giants: 2010, 2012, 2014,

- Position players: Buster Posey, Pablo Sandoval, Brandon Belt (2012, 2014), Brandon Crawford (2012, 2014), Joe Panik (2014)
- Starting pitchers: Matt Cain, Tim Lincecum, Madison Bumgarner
- Relief pitcher: Brian Wilson (2010), Sergio Romo (2012)

### Kansas City Royals: 2014–2015

- Position players: Lorenzo Cain, Alex Gordon, Mike Moustakas
- Starting pitcher: Yordano Ventura
- Relief pitcher: Greg Holland, Kelvin Herrera

### Los Angeles Dodgers: 2017–2018

- Position players: Cody Bellinger, Corey Seager (2017), Joc Pederson, Yasiel Puig
- Starting pitchers: Clayton Kershaw, Hyun-Jin Ryu, Walker Buehler (2018)
- Relief pitcher: Kenley Jansen

In 2017 Charlie Morton, a starting pitcher working in relief, got the last out for the Astros. That is just the same as Madison Bumgarner, who got the last out for the Giants in 2014, and Randy Johnson, who got the last out of the top of the ninth for the Diamondbacks before the walk-off win in the bottom half of the ninth inning in 2001. This is not a new thing in playoff baseball; teams will find a way to get their best pitcher on the bump in crucial situations. In 1967 Bob Gibson got the last out for the Cardinals in Games 1, 4 and 7. He just happened to start those games as well.

I acknowledge that there has been a bit of a changing of the guard and that there are some things being done and thought about differently in the game now than there was before. The new school has certainly made contributions to better the game of baseball, but I don't believe it has made as many new contributions as some in this group claim or believe. Some of the new thinking is based on fancy numbers, phrases, blanket statements, and a one-size-fits-all mentality that doesn't accurately reflect the reality of the game. There seems to be a need to measure everything now, but some of these new measurements and statistics are confusing because they're based on complicated formulas and have questionable results.

Expansion has happened in baseball and will happen again. Every time there has been expansion, the word *diluted* has been used when talking about the talent and play on the field. If thirty teams turn into thirty-two teams in the next possible phase of growing baseball, the pool of opening day big leaguers will go from 750 to 800 players—if each roster stays at twenty-five men. These added players will be AAA players or come from other baseball leagues around the world. Either way, they'll be really good players but maybe not quite big league caliber players yet. This will result in a bit of a watering down of the talent pool, but most of these new guys won't be the big players on their team. They will probably serve as role players, so they should be able to fit in and do the job they are asked to do. To begin the 2019 season, all thirty teams started the year with an active twenty-five–man roster. That's 750 big league players, with a few getting the opening day nod because of an injury to an established big leaguer. But all in all, the large part of this group is that of big league players. Not everyone who plays baseball can say that. There is a finite number of players who can claim to be part of this exclusive group.

Over the years, this number has gone up as teams have been added to the league, but successful expansion should only happen when the player pool is ready to take it on. I understand the business of baseball and acknowledge that generating revenue is important, but in a perfect world the product on the field is the most important thing to consider when growing the number of teams and players. If you were to double the amount of teams, the watering down would be very apparent.

I believe this watering down is happening in the baseball commentary being produced 24/7 in this new media age. Having baseball available all the time isn't a problem, but it seems like with all the different outlets and ways for the fan to access baseball, we've doubled or even tripled the number of voices being heard. If I stay with the premise that there is a finite number of major league players, can't I also make the assumption that there should be a finite number of people qualified to speak about the game professionally? I say yes, simply because in all areas or professions that require a certain level of expertise, there is a finite number or at the very least, a certain number of "grade A" players in the field they represent. Bs and Cs naturally follow.

Bringing the game to the people is great, but the baseball fan who consumes baseball all the time through a variety of media outlets should be aware that everything they hear or see might not be accurate or even relevant. Things are said and terms are used now by watered-down voices that are then repeated by other watered-down voices. I believe that these new voices along with the proliferation of outlets and platforms delivering these messages are sending a landslide of false narratives in their baseball coverage.

In 1988, I finished second among American League
second basemen in double plays turned with 110.

If you need a new roof, you call a roofing company. You wouldn't just trust anyone to do the job. You certainly wouldn't trust someone who has never been on a roof. Being able to see damage from the ground level is one thing, but it doesn't compare to seeing the damage from the roof. Most roofs are different; therefore there is no single way to fix every roof, just like there is no single way to play baseball.

Being able to regurgitate a fancy phrase or an anagrammed statistic shouldn't make anyone an expert on baseball, though many nonexperts may be qualified to speak on the game if they put their time in. I could play a thousand hours of *Call of Duty* and get pretty good at it. This gaming experience would allow me to become familiar with many different types of weapons modeled after the real things. But possessing this knowledge without ever firing the real thing and understanding what that is like cannot make me an expert on anything military. The same goes for baseball.

This book's purpose is to look at the so-called new and improved perspectives on the game and point out what works and what doesn't. Baseball common sense will be this book's main focus as we break down the similarities and differences between the new school of thought and the old school. There is and always will be room in this game for learning and improving, but it's important to bear in mind that new isn't necessarily true, and old doesn't necessarily mean wrong or outdated. The goal is to strike a balance.

If I were to tell you to think of a mousetrap, you will probably have a mental picture of a device that has a flat wooden base and a spring-loaded lever that slams shut as a result of a baited trigger being tripped. This picture in your mind will likely look a lot like the device invented by James Henry Atkinson in 1897. How many people have tried to build a better mousetrap since then? If you have a mouse problem today, you go to your local hardware store and pick up one of those tried and true, old school rodent elimi-nators. You then load the trap with either cheese or peanut butter and place it in the area of the mouse droppings. Within one or two days, there's no more mouse problem. The mousetrap and the game of baseball are both tried and true. Can we tweak things a bit? Sure. But the basic design is something that has stood the test of time and will continue to do so.

Bill's BlackBoard was created in 2016, giving me the ability to break down the complex into simple baseball terms

# CHAPTER 1

# CAL RIPKEN SR.

Whenever the name Ripken is mentioned, the first thing that comes to most people's minds is the Hall of Famer, Cal Ripken Jr. I get this and completely understand it. Cal Jr. is one of baseball's all-time greats. The "Iron Man" broke Lou Gehrig's consecutive games-played streak back in 1995. One of the more popular players in the game's history, Jr. had the fifth highest voting percentage (98.5 percent) of anyone ever elected by the Baseball Writers of America into the National Baseball Hall of Fame.

There were three of us who wore the Ripken name on the back of a major league uniform, but Cal Jr. certainly wore it the best and shined the brightest. His accomplishments on the field and the way he handled those accomplishments off the field secured the legacy of the Ripken name in baseball forever.

This is where Cal Sr. comes in. Dad was a baseball lifer, spending thirty-six years in the Baltimore Orioles organization as a minor league player and manager and as a major league scout, coach, and manager. When Sr.'s minor league playing days got cut short due to a pretty severe shoulder injury, the Orioles organization thought he would be a perfect fit as a player-manager. That's how in 1961, at the ripe old age of twenty-five, Cal Sr. found himself in Leesburg, Florida, and in charge of a group of young men nearly the same age as he was, trying to still play through his injury and continue his career while providing for a family with two kids and a third on the way. That would make any man grow up quickly.

Here's Sr. managing the Orioles' Class-A affiliate Miami Marlins in 1967.

But Dad was used to that. Fourteen years earlier, at age eleven, he lost his father in a car accident. Despite having two older brothers in Oliver and Bill, Dad still had some family responsibilities to take care of, because that was just the way it was back then. In a sense, that's the same thing that was going on in Leesburg that year. Sure there were probably older or more experienced men who could have taken on that responsibility, but they asked for Cal Sr. to do it—and he did.

Part of those responsibilities included filling out nightly reports on what he had seen from that night's game, on every player at every position. At that time, minor league managers weren't given big coaching staffs, if they were given any staff at all. All the manager had to work with in most cases was a pitching coach. So it was Sr.'s job to give the organization his thoughts on whether a player was improving or regressing. Were the errors being made because of poor fields or bad fundamentals? Was the hitter adjusting? Was the pitcher developing his second or third pitch? All of that was in his nightly report.

There are similarities between what Sr. was doing then and what men and women fresh out of college, writing nightly reports for the major league organizations they are a part of, are doing today. But some of these people are doing it from computers in the press box or from offices miles away. Since it was 1961, Sr. did not have the benefit of having the game loaded onto a laptop to watch over and over with pauses and slow motion features. While managing the game he took notes on every player's performance. He would write down key moments of the game on 3x5 index cards. These cards were then left on his desk for the next day. When players filtered in, these cards would match up with the corresponding players and a five-minute meeting would occur to either reinforce or correct something Sr. had observed in the previous night's game.

Sr. was feeling it, seeing it, and living it. His nightly reports were being told to then Orioles farm director Harry Dalton and future Hall of Fame general manager Lee McPhail and having major influence in determining a player's future with the Orioles organization.

Player development is about just that: *player development*. Learning as you go along, learning through experiences, and making adjustments are all a part of the process in rising through the minor league system to become an everyday big league player. Sr.'s job was to help these guys do it. Having the next day's starting pitcher on the top step right next to Sr., charting the game's every pitch, was a great learning tool for the young pitchers. It may not have been the most glamorous job, but it forced them to really watch the game. The weaknesses of the opposing hitters unfolded as the game went along. You didn't have to wait until the next day, when the statistics or analytics were compiled, to see it. The information was quite accurate the next day, I'm sure, but it wasn't any more in-depth than what the "charting pitcher" and Sr. learned from watching every pitch.

Would my dad's job have been a lot easier if he had access to the information we have today? Maybe. It's not a slam-dunk to say yes, though. There is simply no substitute for the experience of living the game every single day. If you gave me a choice between a multitude of analytical information or a highly qualified old school baseball man to determine if a minor league player will make it to the big leagues, I'd choose the baseball man every time.

The clout my father had in the Orioles organization at such a young age also tells you about what the responsibilities of a minor league manager were like back in the day. Dad oversaw every aspect of his team. Who did the early work? What were the batting practice groups? Who played? When did the starting pitcher come out? When and where is the bus stopping for a meal? Who

Here's Sr. with his trusty fungo before a spring training game in Miami.

drives the bus? (Back in 1960 it was him. When Earl Weaver, then the manager of the Fox Cities Foxes, fired the bus driver, Sr. drove the bus the last six weeks of the season.)

Overseeing everything with a coaching staff of one means that Dad was the team's hitting coach, base-running coach, infield instructor, outfield instructor, and his own quality-control coach. Sr. had the ability to help any player on the baseball field. As a catcher, he had the game in front of him. As a manager from the top step of the dugout, it was a little of the same and a little bit different. Being the third base coach (as managers in the minor league often were) also gave him a different perspective, which enabled him to zero in and focus on specific players and situations during the course of a game. These two views coupled with all of his responsibilities shaped Sr. into the baseball man he became.

There may have been guys who were better at instruction in specific areas of the game, but there was no one better equipped to teach the game of baseball overall.

Before the changing of the guard in major league front offices, minor league managers wielded power within their organizations. Dad's team was his to run. He was given certain goals to achieve out of spring training, but he had full reign over executing the plan to get these goals done.

One of the main goals of a minor league manager, then and now, is to develop prospects to become the big league players of the future. In Sr.'s day, certain players were designated as the Orioles' future players and were treated as such. Other players were thought of as possible big league players but perhaps not with the Orioles. The rest of the guys were thought of as good minor league players, and their place in the system was to be the supporting cast for the prospects. But at any time during the season something could happen that might make Sr. change his mind about the classification of any player. The organization had the faith in Dad and in his abilities as an evaluator and a baseball man to give him license to make these determinations, even in the case of high draft picks. In the interest of developing the future Orioles, the best lineup sometimes didn't play every night. This led to some losses as the early part of the season unfolded, but Dad had his eye on the bigger picture. And if Dad and the organization were right in targeting these prospects, they found that the second half of the season went better as the prospects learned and progressed as expected. Winning wasn't everything, especially early in the season; winning became a part of the second half of the season simply because the prospects performed as expected. It's interesting to think about how an established AA player who could help a team win a few more games than a younger, less experienced player could might find himself surpassed at season's end by that younger prospect. This type of managing was what Sr. did best.

One night in 1971, Tom Walker—pitching for my dad's team in Fort Worth, Texas—threw a fifteen-inning no-hitter, with 176 pitches thrown. I will repeat that: *176 pitches thrown.* After the fourteenth inning, even Dad reached a point where he said to Tom, "I can't send you out there for the fifteenth." Tom responded, "We score one here, let me finish." Enos Cabell hit a two-out double, scoring Mike Reinbach for a 1-0 lead. Walker went back out and retired the side in order to earn his fifteen-inning no-no.

The present-day minor league manager might use between six and eight different pitchers to throw 176 pitches on a given night. This is because front offices now mandate pitching rotation by the day. No matter the score or game situation, four different pitchers will take the ball simply because it's their scheduled day on the mound. The minor league manager's job today is different from that of his predecessors in many ways, and this is one of the most glaring. Front-office execs—guys who are often not even located in the same area code as the minor league teams they oversee—are setting lineups and dictating the number of innings a given player may play at each position. And if the goal is to breed a winning culture while developing players, that kind of input conflicts with the achievement of those goals. Somehow, we have gone from minor league managers like my dad having control over everything to a situation in which they control very little. And I would argue that organizations are worse off as a result.

Sr.'s knowledge and expertise helped carve out one of the most successful runs in major league history. From the time my dad first took over in Leesburg, Florida in 1961, to when he was let go by Baltimore in April 1988, the Orioles posted the best record in baseball and won six American League pennants and three World Series. I'm not saying that he should get all of the credit, but the influence he had on the young players rising through the organization helped set the Orioles up for that run of success. While the core players on other World Series teams had their own influencers, those on the Orioles were certainly shaped by Sr. In the minor leagues, he managed and developed a number of future big league players, from my Hall of Fame brother to other Hall of Famers like pitcher Jim Palmer and first baseman Eddie Murray. My dad also had his hand in developing solid major leaguers such as Don Baylor, Bobby Grich, Doug DeCinces, Al Bumbry, Enos Cabell, Andy Etchebarren, Mark Belanger, and pitchers Dean Chance and Mike Flanagan. Even though some of those players made their names outside of Baltimore, the Orioles organization considered it a win whenever players became solid major leaguers.

A true coach's job is to take what he is given to work with and make it better. Sr. did this with both Cal Jr. and me. In Cal Jr.'s case, there was a little bit more to work with. Sr. had a huge hand in shaping and influencing him into the Hall of Famer he became. Jr. probably would have played in the big leagues without Dad's influence, but I do not believe he would have become the "Iron Man" or Hall of Famer he did without it.

## CAL RIPKEN JR.—CAREER STATISTICS

- 19-time American League All-Star
- 1982 American League Rookie of the Year
- 1983 World Series champion
- 2-time American League MVP (1983, 1991)
- 2-time Gold Glove winner at shortstop (1991, 1992)
- 8-time Silver Slugger recipient
- .276 career batting average
- 3,184 career hits (16th all time)

- 431 career home runs (most by a shortstop with minimum 75% games played at the position)
- 603 doubles (16th all time)
- 1,695 RBI (most by a shortstop with minimum 75% games played at the position)
- 5,168 total bases (17th all time)
- Major league record 2,632 consecutive games played

It was a little bit different for me, as I didn't have the size or ability my big brother had. Sr.'s honesty and good old-fashioned "matter-of-fact" style was just what I needed. His advice to "worry about yourself" and "do what you can do" allowed me to take what I had and turn it into a twelve-year career in the big leagues. Considering that the average length of a major league career is 5.6 years, I'd say that's pretty good.

My old-school beliefs can be directly tied to Cal Sr. His no-nonsense approach to doing things was evident both on the baseball field and in his everyday life. Sr.'s influence on me will be scattered throughout this book, as every suggestion he offered about the game of baseball or about doing household chores was backed by his experience and common sense. His second-to-none overall knowledge of the game of baseball combined with his ability to break down the complex and make it simple to understand made him who he was. There's a right way and wrong way to go about your business, whether in school, work, or play. That was Sr. The impact he had on me, both as a ballplayer and as a man, cannot be overstated.

# CHAPTER 2

# THE RIPKEN WAY

Thinking back to all of Dad's years in uniform and all the times he mentored someone, whether in the sport or not, he always had a method to his madness. "The Oriole Way" was entrenched in Cal Sr., and no one was prouder to put on the uniform or to be a part of the Baltimore Orioles organization than he was. Consistency, fundamentals, and attention to detail were some of the pillars of the organization, and Dad was one of the best foot soldiers that the organization ever had. He was always willing to roll up his sleeves and get his hands dirty with good old-fashioned hard work. Doing this as a minor league manager was probably where he had his greatest impact on players. This is not to say that his impact wasn't felt at the big league level, but catching players early in their development and setting the groundwork for their future success is very important, and I believe no one was better at doing that than Sr. was.

The Ripken way was born out of all of Sr.'s years in a model organization, when he was helping to develop major league players. The story is that Eddie Murray and Mike Flanagan were once asked about the Oriole Way in an informal locker room conversation, and their response revolved heavily around Cal Sr. They felt that he was a driving force for promoting the Oriole way of doing things, and the pride in doing so put him at a level above anyone else except for Earl Weaver. Dad took a lot of pride in running the big league camp for Weaver, whom he greatly respected, at the beginning of spring training. He was the mouthpiece for the organization, not publicly, but to the players coming up through the system. These players were the ones who would use the term *the Ripken Way* as far as it related to learning baseball.

We lost Dad back in 1999, so Cal and I created the Cal Ripken Sr. Foundation. Ripken Baseball was already in its early stages. These two organizations are very different, but both needed some rules of the road to be applied to them. We knew what Sr. was about, and we knew what he did and how he did it. So to honor him while trying to be successful with the foundation and Ripken Baseball, we came up with what we believe are some pillars of our own to define the Ripken Way. We believe these four pillars capture the essence of Sr. and are easy to explain by employing one of Dad's strongest suits: common sense.

## 1. KEEP IT SIMPLE

Sometimes the most complex things are complex because we make them that way. Dad broke down things into simple forms. "Take care of the little things, and you will never have a big thing to worry about" was one of his favorite sayings. In baseball, a pitcher giving up a hit or walking a batter or his defense making an error behind him are three little things. If these little things happen in succession, you could be staring at bases loaded with no outs, leading eventually to a big thing. All three things happen in the game frequently, but by taking care of or minimizing the little things the best you can, you cut down the likelihood of big things taking place.

If you're protecting a one-run lead in the top of the ninth and there are runners on first and third with one out, a simple ground ball double play ends the game. This is a perfect example of breaking down the complex to the simple. If the shortstop thinks about the big picture of getting two outs and takes for granted his two parts of the play, he might encounter issues. His parts are catching it and throwing it, and the better he does his two parts, the better the second baseman can do his two parts of catch and throw. If the second baseman executes well, the first baseman is left with his one part of the game-ending play by catching the baseball. This is a great play to be a part of, but understanding this complex play to end a game is nothing more than five simple parts: catch-throw-catch-throw-catch.

A friend of mine was coaching a ten-and-under (10u) team at a fall tournament at my complex in Aberdeen, Maryland; teams that play fall tournaments play up in the next age group in an effort to get a jump on the next baseball season. A 10u team playing as an eleven-and-under (11u) team is introduced to our rules for that age group. These include the fifty-foot pitching distance and seventy-foot base distances, along with base runners leading and stealing the way baseball is played at the highest levels. Ten-year-old baseball at our three complexes in Myrtle Beach, Pigeon Forge, and Aberdeen is the last age group to play on the forty-six-foot pitching and sixty-foot base distances.

My friend called me and asked if I could work with his team's pitchers on their slide steps. I responded, "Why?"

"This leads-and-steal baseball is different," he said, "and we gave up a lot of runs in our first game played with the new rules."

"How'd the runners get on base before they scored runs?"

"Well, we walked a few, made a few errors, gave up some steals, and a few wild pitches allowed some runs to score. They really didn't hit us that well but we gave up a lot of runs."

"We don't need to work on slide steps; we need to work on throwing more strikes and spend a little time with the fielders on the bigger field to get them used to that," I said. Would working with his pitchers on a slide step have helped? Maybe, but working on throwing strikes and working on fielding made more sense to me.

## 2. EXPLAIN THE WHY

Being able to teach is an important part of coaching baseball. Telling someone to do something is not teaching; it is simply telling. Explaining why someone should do something is teaching. If the whys are sound and learning is taking place, the successes will follow. In the younger age groups of youth baseball, suggestions from the stands are often thrown out in an effort to help the participants. One of the most used verbal commands directed at young batters is "Get your elbow up." I've heard this said many times but I've never heard anyone explain why the batter should actually do this. I'm not sure there is a reason why, but it might be the most used "teaching" term in youth baseball. Some hitters do have a raised back elbow and some hitters don't. The hitters who do have a higher back elbow may set their grip and their hands first, and then once they get into their stance the elbow rides high because it feels comfortable to them. Comfort is one of the most important things in a stance. Having a youngster force his elbow up without ever making a connection or knowing a reason why is more than likely not a good idea.

We've all played the dictator game. When a child asks why, sometimes the answer is "Because I said so." I believe parents have earned the right to say "Because I said so" from time to time. As parents our job is to care for and look after our kids and keep them safe, and in doing these things to the best of our ability, we sometimes become dictators in our household. As a parent I'm guilty of that for sure.

Baseball coaches, even old school ones, can't be dictators. As a baseball instructor I do play the guy in charge, but I also have a reason for everything I've ever asked a player to do on the baseball field. I consider myself a teacher. Not to the extent of Cal Sr., but I'm working on it. He was in the teaching game for a long time. Baseball coaches should want their players to ask why. Having those conversations is how learning takes place, whether the player is ten years old or twenty-five years old. A good baseball coach will always have the answer to the whys. Those who don't are not true teachers of the game and will not achieve the full buy-in of their players.

# 3. CELEBRATE THE INDIVIDUAL

No two people are alike, including identical twins. I believe we all know this. For some reason baseball men can lose sight of this very simple observation every now and then. My brother may have assumed more intentionally different stances at home plate than any other major league player in history. I say intentional only to point out that I don't believe anyone can stand at home plate six hundred–plus times a year exactly the same way every time. His stance changes were of his own design. He won an MVP in 1983 with a slightly closed, narrow-based, and very upright stance. He also won an MVP in 1991 with a straight, slightly wider-based, much more crouched stance. These two examples should tell you there isn't just one way to get things done. Jr. probably had at least five really different stances that he used for extended periods of time, and he made a large number of subtle tweaks off of those. He was never afraid to make adjustments at the plate if it meant making himself more comfortable.

My big brother Cal, a two-time American League MVP, was never afraid to make adjustments at the plate if it meant making himself more comfortable.

There are no two hitters in baseball who have an identical stance or swing. There may be similarities in a few that are really close, but generally speaking major league hitters are more different in things they do at home plate than they are similar. What do hitters have in common? They all assume a stance that is comfortable to them. They all have some negative movement—like a snake recoiling before a strike—before the swing starts. When hitting a double in the gap, they all barrel up the baseball. They all have a follow through. These are some basic fundamentals, but every hitter does them in their own way.

Trying to imitate someone's swing is a hard thing to do, as I believe most hitters' swings have been their natural swings since they were ten or twelve years old. Trying to hit like someone else or coaching all hitters to try to hit the same way is probably not going to work, though some coaches, like Charlie Lau and Walt Hriniak, did have some success doing that back in the day.

Different sizes, strengths, skill sets, and natural abilities keep any two hitters from being the same. An individual who can do certain things well should work on perfecting those things moving forward. "Work on your weakness" is a popular idea, but I prefer perfecting your strengths. This is a possibility for every individual in baseball and in life.

## 4. MAKE IT FUN

Having fun is important no matter what you are doing. It doesn't have to be laugh-out-loud fun, but it has to be enjoyable on some level if we expect to do it well. It doesn't take a genius to realize that having fun doing something allows us to succeed at a higher rate than if we are miserable while doing the same task or job. Dad had a saying: "Two things you never do on a baseball field: yawn or laugh. Nothing is ever boring and nothing is ever funny." While on the surface that might seem to contradict the "fun" pillar in our definition of the Ripken Way, don't let the verbiage fool you. No one enjoyed putting the uniform on more than my father did. His idea of fun in baseball was getting after it day after day to try and get better. Getting better meant more success, and more success led to more enjoyment or fun. You wouldn't see him belly laughing on the field very often, as he took this game and his job very seriously, but make no mistake about it, he had fun when he was wearing that uniform. In today's game guys like the Cardinals' Paul Goldschmidt and the A's Marcus Semien project a similar intensity, and both guys enjoy the game as much as anyone.

In baseball, especially youth baseball, the fun should be ever present. Drills are an important part of practice as repetition of specific skills are needed, but how do we do these things while keeping kids engaged in the sometimes slow-moving sport of baseball? We can insert fun. An outfield drill of catching fly balls over the shoulder can have an element of fun by having a coach or an instructor throwing touchdown passes to the kids. A football with no gloves or a baseball with gloves can be used—it's the narrative and the fun the coach puts into it that matters. Having fun during drills will keep the kids engaged longer, but it's not just about the fun part. The coach doesn't even throw the pass unless the outfielder performs the proper steps before going after the ball. The proper steps for an outfielder going back on a ball are a drop step followed by a crossover step and then going after the ball. If the first two steps don't happen, the pass isn't thrown. This way kids will work on proper footwork while having fun.

I've never seen a kid really like hitting off a tee, so how do we engage these kids so they want to do it? Hitting off a tee is very important to the development of a young player's swing, especially in terms of negative movement. So to get them to do it we insert fun. If we're at a hitting facility in an indoor cage, using some sort of target can be an effective way to get the kids' attention. Competitions with kids are always a good idea to help keep the kids engaged. Hitting targets or using point systems for hitting different sidewalls of the netting can be put into place. Hitting line drives back up the middle in any batting drill is never a bad idea and is probably one of the better fundamental things a hitter can do. Integrating some creativity by merging fun and fundamentals into drills and practices will go a long way to fight the boredom that some kids experience. Having one kid hit while the rest of the team stands in the field doesn't work.

I believe these four pillars can span across many things in life as well as the baseball field. Dad always said that everything you do in life you do in baseball, and everything you do in baseball you do in life. So much of what I have learned from this game has applied to my life outside of it, whether it's been at work, as a parent, or in anything else I do. And for that I will always be grateful.

Playing with my brother and for my dad was a truly special experience.

# CHAPTER 3

# PITCH FRAMING

Pitch framing tries to measure a catcher's ability to receive a pitch and a get a strike called on that pitch. This is a little hard for me to understand. I know from watching the game that one catcher can do a better job at this than another can. He might look more relaxed and smoother behind the plate than other catchers do, but does that mean he should get more strikes called on close pitches? A strike should be a strike no matter how it is caught, and the same goes for a ball.

One catcher catching a pitch better than another catcher and getting that pitch called a strike does make a little sense, though. So does one catcher completely butchering a close pitch and forcing the umpire to call it a ball. These two scenarios have some merit, but if we really examine the pitch itself and not the catcher catching it, some of that merit goes away. How does it look? Looking right is one thing, but whether it is an actual strike or ball is the main thing.

A catcher catches the ball several feet away from the front edge of home plate and the front side of the hitter. These two reference points mark the strike zone. So if a thrown pitch actually crosses through the strike zone and then travels several feet more before the catcher catches it, the catcher himself should be irrelevant with regard to the pitch being called a strike or not.

There are many things that factor into a catcher's performance. Some can be measured and some can't. Throwing out base runners can be converted into an understandable percentage. This number does not take the pitcher into account, though. Some are slow and some are quick in their delivery to home plate. The catcher can do everything right during a stolen base attempt, but if the pitcher doesn't give him a chance, it won't matter. The number also doesn't take the speed of the base runner into account, or the jump he gets, or the location of the pitch. If the ball is in the dirt and a guy like the Royals' Whit Merrifield is on the base paths, it doesn't matter how good of an arm the catcher has.

How a catcher handles an entire pitching staff is very hard to measure. Connecting with each individual on a pitching staff on a personal level is integral to their performance as a battery. Defensively minded and skilled catchers are certainly valuable assets to their teams, but trying to assign a number in this category seems like a little bit of a reach to me. Yadier Molina of the Cardinals has been among the league's top ten catchers in fielding percentage in eight of the past ten years, but he rarely ranks among the top pitch framers.

As a matter of fact, I believe the catcher may be one of the least important factors in whether a pitch is called a strike. By my count there are six other factors that come into play before the catcher, and yet pitch framing points solely to the catcher and doesn't take anything else into account.

## SIX REASONS A PITCH IS CALLED A STRIKE OR BALL

1. **It is a strike or a ball:** If the pitch is center-cut in the "K-Zone," the umpire will call it a strike. On the other hand, if the pitch is thrown fifty-eight feet into the dirt, the umpire will rule it a ball.

2. **Pitcher:** A pitcher who has better control and is more often pitching the ball around the strike zone will get the benefit of the doubt regarding close pitches more often than a pitcher who pitches (or throws) wild will. Cy Young pitchers such as Zack Greinke, Corey Kluber, Justin Verlander, and Jacob deGrom get more borderline

As the all-time strikeout king, Nolan Ryan, pictured here as a member of the Houston Astros, didn't need the benefit of the doubt, but sometimes he got it anyway.

pitches called strikes over the course of a game than guys like Gio Gonzalez or Julio Teherán do. A more established veteran pitcher will also get more strikes called on close pitches than a rookie will on those same close pitches. Despite the fact that Nolan Ryan holds the all-time record for walks, "Big Tex" would more often than not get a close pitch called a strike by the home plate umpire, especially later in his career, because of his "stature." Long-time American League umpire Durwood Merrill was known for being an admirer of the seven-time no-hit thrower.

3. **Hitter:** A hitter with a good reputation for knowing the strike zone will get close pitches called balls more often than a free-swinging

The Reds' Joey Votto gets the benefit of the call on
close pitches more than most hitters in the game do today.

hitter with a reputation for chasing pitches out of the zone will. Today, we see hitters like Joey Votto, Mike Trout, and Anthony Rizzo treated better on close pitches than others are. Back in the day Wade Boggs and Frank Thomas also received the benefit of the doubt from umpires on borderline pitches. Similar to the pitcher, an established big league hitter gets more close pitches called in his favor than the rookie or less tenured player does.

4. **Score/situation of the game:** The score of the game is certainly a factor in determining whether close pitches are called strikes or balls. How many times have you seen a borderline pitch called a strike late in a no-hitter or perfect game bid? Similarly, you'll see an increase in strikes called on close pitches late in games that have a lopsided score. This happens at every level of baseball, and it's been that way for a long time.

5. **Stadium:** The stadium in which the game is being played plays a factor as well. Some ballparks, like Yankee Stadium and Fenway Park, carry reputations for having passionate fan bases. The combination of storied, winning franchises and rabid fans sometimes plays into the outcome of a strike or ball getting called at an important juncture in a game.

6. **Umpire:** Some umpires simply call more strikes on borderline pitches than others do, hence the phrases "pitcher's umpire" and "hitter's umpire." Some umpires can get more wrapped up in the emotion of the game situation than others do. Some umpires get caught up in the idea that a game is going on too long, and by expanding the strike zone, they think, "I can speed things up a bit."

Now it's time to consider the catcher. There are guys who receive the baseball very well. Other guys have hands that are a bit harder and don't look so good receiving the pitch. In either case, whether a strike is missed and called a ball or a strike is called when it should have been called a ball, it's the umpire that we should be evaluating. Stealing a pitch by good presentation is something that does happen, but can we really measure this accurately with statistics? Consider the list below. Which comes first, the chicken or the egg? Some of the catchers on the list have caught All-Stars, are Cy Young Award-winners, and are World Series MVPs. It's not a coincidence that catching for elite pitchers with great command will place a catcher high on the frame rate list.

### HIGHEST FRAME RATE AMONG CATCHERS 2013–2018

| | | |
|---|---|---|
| Yasmani Grandal | Padres, Dodgers, Brewers | 121.62 |
| Buster Posey | Giants | 95.49 |
| Tyler Flowers | White Sox, Braves | 82.62 |
| Martín Maldonado | Brewers, Angels, Astros Royals, Cubs | 69.59 |
| Mike Zunino | Mariners, Rays | 62.04 |

I'm not saying that these guys aren't good at their craft. I'm simply pointing out there are a number of things to consider other than the catcher's *slight-of-hand* ability.

Watch your next baseball game with these things in mind. I'll guarantee some of the above will present itself to you. A strike being called because of the framing of the catcher is not really the norm. I've seen games in which a catcher may have a couple of passed balls, questionable wild pitches, and a cross up or two. Lapses such as these lead me to believe that this catcher can't be a good pitch framer. And if he scores well in this category, it may well have to do with some of the other factors listed above.

I value a catcher who keeps passed balls, wild pitches, and cross ups to a minimum. Catchers that don't allow base runners to gain

Yasmani Grandal of the Milwaukee Brewers has by far the
highest frame rate among major league catchers since 2013.

an extra ninety feet on their watch are also valuable. These things
are a part of the pitcher-catcher relationship, and if done well, it
reflects an attention to detail and dedication to his everyday role.
Show me a guy who blocks nearly every ball in the dirt and keeps
runners from advancing, and I'll show you a guy who also receives
pitches well. No pitch framing numbers needed here.

# CHAPTER 4

# LAUNCH ANGLE

L aunch angle is a popular catchphrase that really took root in baseball broadcasts starting in 2018. As the game digs deeper into new statistics, the term *launch angle* has dominated the baseball landscape as much as any other term or phrase has. This new measurable has some people assuming that it's the swing itself that's being measured. But a better way of looking at launch angle is to rename it or think of it as an "exit angle," because the angle of the ball off the bat is what's really being measured.

Some examples could be:

**90°**—Pop up to catcher
**57°**—Fly out to center field
**26°**—Home run
**17°**—Double in the gap
**2°**—Lineout
**-11°**—Ground ball base hit
**-23°**—Ground ball to shortstop
**-63°**—Swinging bunt hit

A completely flat or level swing can result in any of the above outcomes. I'm not saying that an uppercut swing can't be used to create a positive launch angle; I am saying that the swing itself is *not* the launch angle.

The following two statements are made on baseball broadcasts fairly regularly. These statements are sometimes made with a complete lack of knowledge regarding this topic.

1. **"He worked on his launch angle."**

   Launch angle is a result, and it is very difficult to work on a result. Do hitters work on hitting doubles or do they work on achieving a repeatable swing that can produce doubles? Most hitters go to the cage and work on something specific. They will work on bottom hand, top hand, stride, catching it out in front, letting it get deep, front side, backside, and other various hitting drills. Launch angle is never mentioned or discussed by the hitter or his hitting coach in these training sessions. When I do hitting segments on air with Hall of Famer Jim Thome, who hit 612 home runs in the major leagues, and Sean Casey, a career .302 hitter, the term is never mentioned either. So I ask: Why is it when a hitter has success that broadcasters say "he must have worked on his 'launch angle'"?

2. **"He improved his launch angle."**

   This one is used all the time, and I have no idea what it means. Whoever makes this statement as a stand-alone remark is simply using it because they heard it somewhere else and didn't have anything else to contribute. My question for the user of this statement is: Did he improve his launch angle by lowering or raising the launch angle?

Let's take a look at the 2018 National League MVP runner-up, Chicago Cubs infielder Javier Báez. The then twenty-five-year-old hit a career-high thirty-four home runs, and many announcers attributed his increase in power to his launch angle. But the statistics speak to the reverse being true.

### JAVIER BÁEZ: 2016–2018

|  | Launch Angle | AVG | SLG% | HR |
|---|---|---|---|---|
| 2016 | 11.4 degrees | .273 | .423 | 14 |
| 2017 | 9.1 degrees | .273 | .480 | 23 |
| 2018 | 9.2 degrees | .290 | .554 | 34 |

Now let's take a look at the 2018 MVP winners in each league. These men were separated by nearly two hundred spots in the "launch angle" rankings, but the player with the lower launch angle hit four more home runs.

### LAUNCH ANGLE AMONG 2018 MVP WINNERS— RANKS AMONG 228 PLAYERS WITH 250 PA

|  | AVG Launch | MLB Rank | 2018 HR Total |
|---|---|---|---|
| Mookie Betts (BOS) | 18.4 degrees | 17th | 32 |
| Christian Yelich (MIL) | 4.7 degrees | 215th | 36 |

In short, there is no magic number or formula for launch angle. It is a completely case-by-case, player-by-player evaluation.

The Cubs Javier Báez hit a career-high thirty-four home runs in 2018,
but could his power surge be attributed to launch angle?

The swing is certainly a major contributor to the launch angle. But as I mentioned earlier, big league hitters have pretty much had the same swings since they were playing youth baseball through high school. One of the reasons these guys were drafted in the first place was because of their swing. If you're drafted because you're better than other players and you enter the minor leagues and continue to progress and develop, there's not really any need to change much. The plan, the approach, and the mental side of hitting can weigh in as much as the swing does regarding how the ball comes off the bat. Hitters have a better chance of changing their thought processes and approaches to hitting than they do changing their swings. If it were as easy as saying "I'm going to the cage to change my swing," every right-handed hitter would look like Mike Trout and every left-handed hitter would look like Ken Griffey Jr. They don't, because it ain't that easy. What's natural for one player might not be natural for another. That's why everyone's stance, set up, swing, and follow through are different.

Picking your spots to catch a few more balls out front, taking advantage of a favorable count, or looking for a certain pitch because you believe there's a pattern to how you're being pitched can lead to a gapper or homer. This thought process, along with your natural swing, may send your launch angle up a notch or two. Using a two-strike approach and telling yourself "Don't strike out" might allow you to use your natural swing while shortening or even eliminating your stride in a "short-to-the-ball" manner like Juan Soto of the Nationals and Cody Bellinger of the Dodgers do so well. This will afford you a much better chance to put the ball into play and avoid a strike out, but the result might be that your launch angle comes down a bit. That said, it can also result in a homer. Sometimes the easy, short swing works in a way that you wouldn't think it would. Trying to force the ball into the air can lead to a higher launch angle, but it may also lead to some bad at bats and some prolonged slumps. The launch angle is talked about in a way that suggests that higher is better, but this is a one-size-fits-all mentality that simply isn't true.

The Pittsburgh Pirates' Josh Bell made a big splash in his first full major league season in 2017, hitting twenty-six homers and driving in ninety runs while hitting .255 to finish third in the voting for National League Rookie of the Year Award behind the Dodgers' Cody Bellinger and the Cardinals' Paul DeJong. His 2018 season didn't quite stack up to his rookie campaign, though. Articles were written pointing to the idea that his struggles could be directly tied to his launch angle. The only problem with that was his launch angle from 2017 to 2018 was roughly the same; in fact it went up from 8.6 to 9.2. That's still below the league average for launch angle, which in 2018 was 11.7, though. I've never heard anyone from the new school say that an improved launch angle is a bad thing.

My point is a simple one: How can a hitter's launch angle even be considered as a possible reason for their struggles at the plate? It really can't. It is a result, but there could be several things to point to prior to the ball coming off the bat. We might as well say that Bell's struggles were a result of him hitting only twelve home

2017 National League Rookie of the Year Cody Bellinger of the Dodgers is one of the game's best two-strike hitters.

runs compared to the twenty-six he hit as a rookie. Does that make any sense? No. As I've said before and will continue to say, the launch angle is a term that sounds catchy, but it's a metric that simply gets overused and is completely misunderstood in a variety of ways. If the ball comes off the bat in a similar direction from one year to another, that tells me that most everything prior to that ball coming off the bat must be pretty similar as well. Everything prior refers to stance, set up, and the swing itself. So what, possibly, could be a real reason for a hitter's struggles?

How about health? Bell did spend some time on the injured list in 2018 with an oblique issue. Let's say that he wasn't quite right physically just before he officially went onto the injured list and tried to play through it. If this is true, everything in the approach and the swing can look pretty similar, but if something, maybe that little extra, isn't there, this could be an issue. The ball may come off the bat in a similar direction but maybe not as hard as it did before. This can certainly change the outcome of a batted ball. So let's take a look at the time spent on the injured list. Usually, what happens first when a player goes inactive because of an injury is rest and treatment by the training staff. That treatment may include some baseball activities, as the body will allow, until the player is ready to rejoin the team's active roster and start playing games again. Some players will push the envelope and try and get back as quickly as they can. This may mean that players play the game with nagging injuries and compromised body parts during the course of a 162-game season. I also know that an oblique injury is one that can linger. Even if there's no pain, the full function of an oblique muscle and the complete strength of the abdominal core returning to a player takes some time. This may be speculation on my part, but it is something that I experienced as a player, and it makes way more sense to me than a bad launch angle as to why someone might struggle.

The Pirates' Josh Bell had a whopping 84 RBIs at the
all-star break in 2019, but only 32 RBIs in the season's second half.

At the 2019 all-star break, Josh Bell ranked among the major league leaders in home runs, extra base hits, and he dominated RBIs with 84! Those are damage numbers that matter. While he wasn't able to maintain that production in the second half as he tried to play through some injuries and the Pirates faded from contention, his launch angle actually increased from 10.9 to 16.8. Still, Bell's performance in the first half of the season established him as one of the game's elite power- and run-producing presences. The second half of 2019 excluded, he's done this while maintaining virtually the same launch angle throughout his short big league career. So if a player like Bell has three years of big league experience and a slightly below-league average launch angle for that timespan, what does launch angle really mean when he's put up the kinds of numbers he has? More importantly, as stated above: How can we possibly attribute any struggles he may have had in '18 to a bad launch angle when it's pretty much been the same year after year?

This persistent misconception, along with using launch angle as a synonym for the swing itself, could prove problematic for young players. There are already enough bad teaching ideas circulating throughout youth baseball, but the misrepresentations of what launch angle is and the impact it has on a hitter's performance could be one of the worst things to enter into the game in a while, especially at the youth level. Having a ten-year-old hitter work on hitting the ball in the air will not help his future chances of playing at a higher level. Encouraging Little Jimmy to hit homers before showing him how to make consistent line drive contact will not bode well for him in the long run. He might not even be capable of reaching the fences anyway. The approach of swinging up on the baseball along with his smaller size and strength compared to the bigger players on his team will lead to no success and certainly no fun. The lazy fly balls and strikeouts that are sure to result from that approach are a recipe for Little Jimmy to leave the game in search of something else where he can enjoy success and have some fun. Hitting line drives and hard ground balls is always the better option with the younger age groups, especially when you consider how many ball fields at that level don't even have outfield fences. The ball will find its way into the air over time, when the young hitter gets a little bit bigger and stronger while figuring out some things on his own.

Coaches, please do not have young kids force the ball into the air! Baseball players and coaches competing at the highest levels of the game should feel responsible for sending out messages that could lead to teaching young players the wrong things. Keep in mind, the "default to launch angle" people are not baseball personnel, generally speaking. They're a group of people—members of the media primarily—who can offer a few things here and there, but they are not the baseball coaches or teachers of the game. Big league hitters have their launch angles discussed by some in the new school just because that's the way it has gone over the last few years, but these same big league hitters go to the cages every day and hit line drive rockets off the back wall of the netting. They do this to work on their swing whether they're using a tee or hitting soft toss. Launch angle is not discussed *at all* during these hitting sessions.

# CHAPTER 5

# SPIN RATE

O ver the last few years the term *spin rate* has been employed frequently during game broadcasts and baseball studio shows. This has led to the assumption that spin rate has a direct effect on whether a pitcher is having success or is struggling. Let's slow that roll a bit.

This is a measure that does have some merit. Let's start with the four-seam fastball. This is a pitch designed to get from point A to point B. Pitchers with good velocity and good spin rate like throwing the high fastball because it fights gravity and stays on a truer plane than fastballs that don't have such a good spin rate. In the old days, we would simply say, "his heater has late life" or "it jumps." But while a higher spin rate on a fastball can certainly contribute to a pitcher's success, it is not imperative to it.

Here's an example: The Yankees' Luis Severino struggled on the mound after July 2018. Through July 1, hitters were hitting only .214 against his fastball, but after July 1 they were hitting nearly .350 against it. So naturally people assumed that his velocity had decreased, his ball didn't have life, or his spin rate had gone down, which it had slightly. It had gone down a measly 14 RPM, and that didn't make Severino's fastball that much easier to hit.

## LUIS SEVERINO FASTBALLS—2018 SEASON

|  | Thru July 1st | After July 1st |
|---|---|---|
| Fastball Usage | 50.4% | 50.5% |
| AVG FB Velocity | 97.8 MPH | 97.4 MPH |
| AVG FB Spin Rate | 2371 RPM | 2357 RPM |
| Opp. AVG on FB | .214 | .347 |

Overall, for the season, Luis Severino ranked eleventh in the majors in spin rate among pitchers with at least 2,250 pitches thrown. Is that the reason he had success in his first eighteen starts of the 2018 season? We clearly see that in his final fourteen starts he had virtually the same velocity and spin rate, but for some reason he was getting hit harder. Obviously, more examination is needed.

Let's tackle this by looking at some other examples. Here are the top five pitchers of 2018 in opponent's average against the fastball and where they rank in spin rate on the fastball.

The Yankees' Luis Severino ranked eleventh in the Majors
in 2018 in spin rate among pitchers with at least 2,250 pitches thrown.

| LOWEST OPPONENT'S AVG ON FOUR-SEAM FASTBALL—2018 SEASON, MIN. 150 PA | | |
|---|---|---|
| | | Spin Rate (MLB Rank) |
| David Price (BOS) | .175 | 2192 RPM (51st) |
| Gerrit Cole (HOU) | .184 | 2372 RPM (10th) |
| Max Scherzer (WSH) | .198 | 2486 RPM (4th) |
| Aaron Nola (PHI) | .206 | 2100 RPM (69th) |
| Julio Teherán (ATL) | .210 | 2270 RPM (33rd) |

*Average spin rate on four-seam fastball in MLB: 2263 RPM

What this table confirms to me is that pitchers who throw strike one and have secondary pitches they can throw for strikes are guys who have success regardless of their spin rate. Price, Cole, and Scherzer consistently throw three pitches for strikes nightly. Strike one has been and always will be the best pitch in baseball.

The curveball has become an interesting study as far as spin rate goes as well. The terminology for a guy with a good curveball has turned into "He can really spin the baseball."

How well can he spin it? Is spinning the baseball the key to an effective curveball? Pitchers such as Chris Stratton of the Giants and Seth Lugo of the Mets ranked number one and two respectively in spin rate with their curveballs over the 2017 and 2018 seasons. These two pitchers are still relatively unknown despite being at the top of that list, though Lugo has developed into a reliable reliever for the Mets in 2019.

Let's do the same exercise for the curveball that we did for the fastball.

| LOWEST OPPONENT'S AVERAGE ON CURVEBALLS AMONG STARTING PITCHERS— 2018 SEASON—MIN. 75 PA ENDING IN PITCH | | |
|---|---|---|
| | | Spin Rate (MLB Rank) |
| Corey Kluber (CLE) | .104 | 2607 RPM (23rd) |
| Blake Snell (TBR) | .126 | 2517 RPM (28th) |
| Charlie Morton (HOU) | .135 | 2923 RPM (4th) |
| Justin Verlander (HOU) | .137 | 2894 RPM (5th) |
| Mike Clevinger (CLE) | .138 | 2194 RPM (54th) |

*Average spin rate on curveball in MLB: 2493 RPM*

I'll guarantee there are pitchers in the minor leagues who have better spin rates on their breaking balls than some of the guys who have had success in the big leagues. Once again, this is a measure that has some merit, but throwing this pitch for a strike while having other pitches that can be thrown for strikes is the key. It's about being a complete pitcher as opposed to a guy who has one dominant pitch, even when that pitch is a hundred mile an hour fastball. Major league hitters can hit hundred mile an hour fastballs when they know they're coming.

It's no surprise to see Justin Verlander's name on the list above. The eight-time all-star might not have the electric fastball he had when he was younger, but he consistently throws four pitches for strikes: a hard four-seam fastball, a slider, a curveball, and a changeup. His ability to throw any of those pitches in any situation is a key reason why, at thirty-six, he's still one of the game's most successful pitchers.

• • •

It's no surprise that the Astros Justin Verlander's curveball,
one of four pitches the eight-time all-star can consistently throw
for a strike, has one of the best spin rates in all of baseball.

The combination of high fastballs with a curveball was also referenced an awful lot during game broadcasts last year. It also seemed to be presented in a way that made it seem like it was a new tool pitchers could use to combat the "launch angle revolution." But this isn't like Neil Armstrong taking his first step on the moon. Pitchers have been throwing the heater-hook combination dating back to the days when the umpire stood behind the mound. This isn't a new concept for pitchers attacking hitters. Pitchers can attack in the following ways: up-down, in-out, and add-subtract. These approaches can be a little cyclical in how they are employed in the game. Back in the day it seemed as if fastball/curveball was the norm. This was followed by the sinker/slider, then the straight change, and then the add/subtract (the fastball-changeup combination). These are still the three most common ways pitchers attack hitters. Pitchers who can use two of these are good, but pitchers who can utilize all three are great. A good spin rate can be beneficial to a pitcher, but it cannot be looked at as the sole reason for one's success or failure.

I would view spin rate as a diagnostic tool for everyone. It's as unique as a fingerprint. The spin rate for every person who throws a baseball is theirs and theirs alone; it's how they throw a ball. In my way of thinking it's best served as a rehabilitation tool for injury. If a healthy pitcher has a ninety-five-mile-per-hour fastball and a spin rate of 2400 RPM but then suffers an arm injury and comes back to pitch with the same velocity but a lower spin rate, he might have a problem. A pitcher can usually find the velocity, but he may be doing something differently to achieve that velocity. If this is the case, he may be putting the health of another body part at risk. This would tell me that his "fingerprint" isn't quite right. He doesn't have the same "free and easy" delivery that he had prior to the injury.

The same could be said for a guy with a good curveball. Comparing a guy's spin rate on his hook pre-injury to post-injury will give you a good idea if he's made it all the way back or not.

# CHAPTER 6

# PITCHING WINS

**M**ost if not all in the analytics community believe that pitching wins simply do not matter. I would prefer their stance to be that pitching wins don't matter as much as they once did. I'm okay with this kind of statement. In yesteryear it was assumed that a starting pitcher's job was to go deep into the game or even finish it. That type of outing is almost gone from the game now, with the exception of a select few pitchers who, on occasion, will go the distance (usually in pursuit of a no-hitter). Hall of Famer Warren Spahn completed 382 games over the course of his twenty-one year major league career, including twelve seasons with at least twenty complete games. But in 2018 eight pitchers tied for the major league lead with a whopping two complete games. Rigid pitch counts and relief specialization have made it so openers and bullpen games are now the norm. If your starter goes at least six innings without surrendering more than three earned runs, he is considered to have delivered a "quality start."

And starters going four and two-thirds but getting hooked despite a lead because of a "high leverage situation" may spell the end of the pitching win as we know it. But let's hold on a second.

Hall of Famer Warren Spahn completed 382 games over the course of his twenty-one year major league career, which included twelve seasons with at least twenty complete games.

I know—and so do other baseball people—that a win-loss record can still paint a picture and possibly tell me something about a pitcher. Part of being a baseball guy is relying on your experience in the game to help put pieces together that you might not have seen before. If I see a pitching matchup in which pitcher A has a 15-5 record and a 3.50 ERA and pitcher B has an 8-10 record with a 3.00 ERA, I can speculate that pitcher A maybe does something really well when the game is on the line compared to pitcher B. Digging into this a little deeper, I also see if the innings pitched, strikeouts, walks, and hits are all relatively close. And if they are I can feel better about my gut reaction, so much so that I might prefer the 3.50 ERA guy over the 3.00 ERA guy.

Digging even deeper through some game logs and finding the critical innings of record, pitcher A doesn't seem to buckle under certain pressures and makes pitches when he absolutely has to. Pitcher B, on the other hand, seems to give up a lot of two-out, two-run knocks when he is trying to hold a one-run lead. Sometimes the runners are on base because of error and those two runs are unearned. Pitcher B's team goes on to lose a bunch of games by one run, though his ERA doesn't suffer much as a result.

This is a completely hypothetical scenario as written, but this type of game situation has occurred before my time in the game, during my time in the game, and happens in today's game. So for this exercise and for the record, I choose pitcher A over pitcher B.

I'm completely okay with how the 2018 National League Cy Young Award voting unfolded. Jacob deGrom had a great year, and the Mets hitters clearly gave him no run support.

• • •

The Mets' Jacob deGrom won the 2018 National League
Cy Young Award despite winning only ten games.

## 2018 NATIONAL LEAGUE
## CY YOUNG AWARD 1-2 FINISHERS

|  | W-L | ERA | IP | H | K/BB |
|---|---|---|---|---|---|
| Jacob deGrom (NYM) | 10-9 | 1.70 | 217.0 | 152 | 269/46 |
| Max Scherzer (WSH) | 18-7 | 2.53 | 220.2 | 150 | 300/51 |

*Jacob deGrom earned twenty-nine of thirty first-place
votes to win the 2018 National League Cy Young Award.*

In 1990, during my time in the game, Bob Welch's twenty-seven wins won him the American League Cy Young Award over Roger Clemens and his 1.93 ERA (and 21-6 record). Wins mattered more back in the day and Welch's twenty-seven wins were the most any pitcher had posted in eighteen years, but it was not as much of a landslide victory as the 2018 National League Cy Young Award race ended up being.

Two points need to be made here: First, Bob Welch clearly played on a very good, pennant-winning Oakland Athletics team, but no one else on the A's had twenty-seven wins. Dave Stewart did post twenty-two wins that year with a 2.56 ERA, but as good as that was, it wasn't twenty-seven. Second, the fact that this race was not a landslide tells me that the voters looked at some other numbers beside the win column.

### 1990 AMERICAN LEAGUE CY YOUNG AWARD 1–2 FINISHERS

|  | W-L | ERA | IP | H | K/BB |
|---|---|---|---|---|---|
| Bob Welch (OAK) | 27-6 | 2.95 | 238.0 | 214 | 127/77 |
| Roger Clemens (BOS) | 21-6 | 1.93 | 228.1 | 193 | 209/54 |

*Bob Welch earned fifteen of twenty-eight first-place votes to win the 1990 American League Cy Young Award.*

I do understand that wins don't paint the whole picture and we should look at them differently, especially now. But completely dismissing or diminishing a guy who has the knack for winning seems a little absurd to me. There are guys in the game who don't have the ancillary numbers that jump off the board at you but find a way to make pitches when they have to. They just find a way to win. Relievers sometimes come in and blow saves and some starters get hurt by their teammates' fielding errors or a lack of run support, but there are some front-line starters who simply refuse to lose.

All statistical categories should come into play when evaluating a pitcher and the W is still a part of this evaluation. It's pretty safe

The Athletics' Bob Welch won twenty-seven games in 1990,
the most in eighteen years. Nobody has won more than twenty-four since.

to say that a pitcher with a record of 18-7 over thirty-three starts and 210 innings had a good year, even if he had what looks like an inflated ERA.

The win might not matter as much as it once did, and I believe everyone is well aware of that. But pitchers who find a way to make the ten to fifteen pitches they absolutely have to at crucial points of the game don't lose. I understand the "win" is sometimes out of the pitcher's control, but I also understand that taking a loss is many times completely within his control.

The starting pitchers that refuse to lose put themselves in a position to win. These pitchers haven't given in to the idea that pitching wins don't matter. I hear about this new pitching philosophy "buy in" going on with certain teams and certain pitchers. Yet I see starting pitchers being removed in the fifth inning with the win on the line, and a clear look of disdain can be seen on their faces. I see starters being removed with an 8.1 or even 8.2 innings pitched with complete games on the line and see that same look. That doesn't seem like true buy-in to me.

Building a team around starting pitchers who want to do their jobs as if it was back in the day is still the best way to establish a winning culture. This has shown itself with the past few World Series winners, including Washington and Houston, and will show itself again in the future ones. There might be an exception or two over the next twenty years, but the teams that have the horses in the rotation will have the flexibility and luxury of a well-rested pen. These teams will also be in the driver's seat as the postseason rolls on.

# CHAPTER 7

# TUNNELING

*T*unneling is the new name used to describe what a pitcher is doing when he is able to throw several different pitches from the same arm slot and release point with the ball staying in a virtual tunnel for a period of time before the different pitches do what they do. A fastball and a slider can't stay in the same tunnel from the pitcher's hand all the way to the catcher's glove, but the longer the two pitches do stay in that tunnel, the chance of deception is higher. If you can't visualize the tunnel concept, think about a pipe stretching from the pitcher's hand at the release point to the catcher's glove. A good four-seam fastball should be able to travel through this pipe from hand to glove. The curveball, slider, split-finger, and change-up cannot make it through the pipe if they do what they're supposed to do. How far within the pipe each pitch can travel before they break or drop from lack of velocity is the important thing. I should have weighed in on this phenomenon three years ago and received credit for naming it "piping."

Tunneling is one of the newer terms in the game, and it hasn't quite hit it as big as some of the others we've discussed in this book. But it is gaining some momentum. It is certainly substantial and it's a real thing, but I believe it is also being sold and received as somewhat of a new invention, which it isn't. By bringing this one to light a little early in the process, I hope to mitigate some of the confusion that will follow as it picks up speed, which it will, as I've been hearing it thrown about more and more. It seems to me when this term gets used, some react as if they've just had their "I should've had a V-8" moment, like a caveman seeing fire for the first time. It seems to be an easy phrase to use whenever a pitcher is having some success. The difference between the very first fire sighting and tunneling, however, is that tunneling has been seen before because it has been around since the game began. But it wasn't cleverly named at first, so some might not have known it existed. Having different pitches that look the same at the release point has always been what the pitcher wanted.

Organizations are now targeting pitchers who can tunnel when looking at amateur players, evaluating free agents, or getting a pitcher in a trade. I believe this should prove to be fairly easy, as almost every pitcher out there has multiple pitches that are thrown from the same release point. Looking for "good tunnel guys" is quicker to say and sounds better than looking for "guys with good stuff who throw all their pitches from the same release point." I'm sure that I could throw a fastball, slider, and change-up from the same release point, but I'm also sure that at age fifty-five my pitches wouldn't be able to get big league hitters out, even if I am flawless with my tunneling.

This new term is emblematic of the ever-present need to measure and name everything in the game. It's amazing to me that Hall of Famer Greg Maddux pitched twenty-three years in the majors without one mention of tunneling. How did he ever get anyone out without knowing about tunneling? I can visualize him facing a left-handed batter right now: He quickly gets ahead of the hitter with a well-executed cut fastball in on the batter's hands, forcing an awkward swing that results in a slow-rolling foul ball to the pull side. With the count at no balls and one strike, Maddux then follows up his cutter with a two-seam fastball that starts in the same location as the first pitch did but instead of cutting in on the left hand hitter, this one comes back to hit the inside corner for strike two. The hitter takes this pitch, as it looked just like the previous pitch that tied him up. With the count 0-2, Maddux tries to finish the hitter off by painting a two-seamer away, hoping he can freeze him and get the rare three-pitch punch-out. The third pitch is thrown with the intent to either hit the corner or miss away. He throws the pitch and just misses off the plate, and the hitter knows it just missed. With the count 1-2 and considering how that count was reached, the possibilities for getting the hitter out with the next pitch are endless. In this particular case, Maddux decides to go with a change-up in the same location as the previous pitch. This pitch is swung at and missed for strike three. The two pitches that started the at bat looked exactly the same coming out of Maddux's hand but had different action. The same goes for the two pitches at the end of the at bat. If Maddux were pitching today he might very well be known as the tunnel king! That was the way Greg Maddux pitched all the time. His deception came from using multiple pitches that looked the same coming out of his hand. His mechanics were sound, he didn't alter his motion or arm slot, and he always seemed to be in control without ever really being a maximum effort guy.

•   •   •

Hall of Famer Greg Maddux was a tunneller before tunneling was a thing.

Deception has always been a part of pitching, and pitchers with more of a textbook look to their mechanics might need to tunnel a bit better than some others who might have more unconventional mechanics. Back in the day Luis Tiant relied on a variety of different arm slots and release points to get hitters out. Throwing different variations of his full repertoire from different arm angles was a big key in his success as a pitcher. A three-time all-star, El Tiante was a master of deception as he used every trick in the book (except tunneling) to upset hitters' comfort and timing. He would sometimes even turn his back to the hitter during his windup to create an edge. The 1994 American League Cy Young

Award-winner, David Cone, was also known to change his pitching motion to create or invent a pitch or two during the course of an at-bat. Hall of Famer Mike Mussina altered his delivery once in a while, especially toward the end of his career when he tinkered with a few more sidearm looks and managed to win twenty games in his final season. The Giants' Johnny Cueto is a contemporary that does his own thing by employing hesitations, quick pitches, body turns, and a variety of different arm angles. These guys purposely did and do different things to gain an advantage, while other pitchers rely on something a little more natural and unforced to gain the advantage of deception.

Height and size fall into the natural category for sure, and the first pitcher that comes to my mind in the area of height is 6'10" Randy Johnson. Johnson's length and very low three-quarter delivery presented challenges for hitters simply because he was so unique. Match that with a mid-nineties-and-above fastball and a sweeping hard slider, two pitches that were as good as anyone else's two-pitch mix. It's easy to see why he ended up in Cooperstown. I don't believe that the word *tunneling* would be used to describe him as much if he were pitching today. His hand position at release was slightly different on his slider than it was on his fastball, and it had to be slightly different for him to get any downward tilt on it. This is because of where his release point was on his fastball. Even though the difference in the release point and hand position may have been a couple of inches on these two pitches, the hitter had no chance of picking out either pitch at real game speed.

The Red Sox's Chris Sale is a guy to watch now. He's not quite as tall as Johnson is (few are), and he doesn't quite drop as low on his release point either, but he has a crossfire delivery in which he steps toward the left-handed hitters' batters box instead of directly toward home plate. This crossfire presents problems for both left-handed and right-handed hitters. Left-handed hitters have to fight the urge to pull off the ball with their front shoulder when starting their swings as a result of Sale's release point, which is literally coming from behind them. Right-handed hitters may have a difficult time picking up the ball as the crossfire delivery hides the ball longer; and the longer it takes to recognize a pitch the harder it is for a hitter to hit it.

I've done many in-depth breakdowns on pitchers since I've been an analyst for the Major League Baseball Network. These have covered a multitude of topics and ideas ranging from one at-bat battles, utilizing the fastball–change-up combination, the utter nastiness of some pitchers' stuff, the scissor effect of the heater-slider combo, the high heater/hook, windups, release points, thought processes, and tunneling, though I didn't call it that. All pitchers go about the art of pitching a little bit differently, yet with similarities of sorts, and guys who have clean mechanics and who basically show you the ball all the way through delivery are probably the guys that tunnel the best. As I've said, this is a real thing and it definitely has its place in the pitching conversation. Just be mindful of matter-of-fact oversimplification when a pitcher appears to be having success because of tunneling. Tunneling will only play a part in a pitcher's success if he throws strikes, has good stuff, and knows when to throw each pitch.

Once again, I give you Greg Maddux.

# CHAPTER 8

# BATTING AVERAGE VERSUS ON-BASE PERCENTAGE

A nother one of the new ways of thinking introduced by the analytics community is its view on the value of batting average compared to on-base percentage. Some in this group have even used the blanket statement, "Average doesn't matter." But would they really take a guy who walks forty times in a hundred at bats and gets zero hits over a guy who gets thirty-five hits and zero walks in those same hundred at bats?

The user of that blanket statement is either showing a complete lack of understanding with regard to baseball, or they're just trying to present themselves as some sort of expert; either option is not good. The old school baseball guy gets frowned upon when he dismisses an analytics guy's ideas because the analytics guy didn't play the game; and I agree that they should be frowned upon, even when what they are saying is true. But where are the frowns when an over-the-top analytics guy speaks and makes a ridiculous statement? It's here; I'm frowning now. Saying that "batting average doesn't matter" simply isn't true, and it's as much of an insult to an old school baseball guy as saying "you didn't play" to an analytics guy. The batting average is the biggest part and walks are the smallest part of on-base percentage. This fact alone should tell you that average matters. More offensive good can happen as a result of a hit instead of a walk. A hit can be a single, double, triple, or home run.

The thought among some of the new school is that a hitter's goal is to not make outs. The player with a .400 on-base percentage makes an out sixty times in a hundred at-bats. The player with a .350 on-base percentage makes an out sixty-five times in a hundred at-bats. If both of these players have thirty hits with similar power numbers, then yes, you prefer the guy who walked ten times instead of five. My gripe is with the blanket statement and the people who have used this statement. We all understand that a higher on-base percentage can be a good thing, but "batting average doesn't matter" is a ridiculous statement. A hitter's goal should be to do what he can to help his team score runs. More runs result from hits than walks.

Here's a case study: Los Angeles Angels outfielder Mike Trout is viewed both by the new school and the old school as the best player in the game today. The two-time MVP's 162-game average stat line per season is .307, 37 HR and 99 RBI. For this exercise let's take twenty of his hits and move them to the walk column. Based on a simple formula, his home run and RBI total go down because twenty hits are removed.

## MIKE TROUT 162-GAME AVERAGE THROUGH 2018

|  | Actual | Case study |
|---|---|---|
| Plate appearances | 711 | 711 |
| At-bats | 589 | 569 |

|                     | Actual | Case study |
|---------------------|--------|------------|
| Hits                | 181    | 161        |
| Walks               | 105    | 125        |
| HR                  | 37     | 33         |
| RBI                 | 99     | 87         |
| **Batting AVG**     | **.307** | **.283** |
| On-base percentage  | .416   | .416       |

Now obviously his on-base percentage stays the same, but his batting average drops twenty-four points. So now is it a slam-dunk argument that Mike Trout is the best player in baseball?

I'm sure that some in the new school won't be fazed by this study, but some might be. The old school would be alarmed if those case study numbers were real; either way Mike Trout would not be the consensus best player in the game. Hits matter. Therefore, average matters too.

One thing managers and pitchers use as a form of strategy is the walk, which is either a pitch-around or intentional. Either way it also still counts toward a player's on-base percentage. During one four-game stretch in May 2016, Cubs manager Joe Maddon used that form of strategy in a series against the Nationals and reigning National League MVP Bryce Harper. During that series, Harper reached base fifteen times. The Cubs walked him thirteen times, four times intentionally, and the Cubs swept the series. Compare that to a four-game series a year later against the Reds when Bryce walked only four times, went seven for seventeen with three homers, and drove in seven runs as Washington won all four games. So would the Washington Nationals prefer the .789 on-base percentage versus the Cubs or the .524 on-base percentage against the Reds? I know one thing: the Cubs preferred the .789 on-base percentage.

The Cubs walked 2015 National League MVP
Bryce Harper thirteen times in a four game series back in 2016.

Passing the baton by taking a walk is good in some cases. Expanding the strike zone and driving in a run should also be looked at as a good thing. There's a fine line between staying within yourself and possibly coming out of your comfort zone to drive in a run. I've seen hitters over the last few seasons who seemed more inclined to stay within their comfort zones rather than overextend themselves due to the increased emphasis on on-base percentage.

All offensive contributions should be considered and measured. I'm not dismissing the walk or on-base percentage, I'm just making a point that hits are better than walks. The numbers being over-examined, created, and adjusted by some in the new school are mind blowing.

I'll say it again: "Pitch it, catch it, and hit it better than the other team and you'll win." Even in today's game, it's still that simple. The only number that truly matters in any baseball game is the score. Score more runs than your opponent does and you win. You score more runs via the hit than the walk.

# CHAPTER 9

# WINS ABOVE REPLACEMENT (WAR)

**W**AR is a metric that has gained popularity over the last decade as another way to analyze players with one singular number. But first, let's consider the definition of WAR. WAR is an acronym for Wins Above Replacement, which means the statistic is an attempt by the sabermetric baseball community to summarize a player's total contributions to his team in one number. According to FanGraphs.com, WAR seeks to answer the question "If this player got injured and his team had to replace him with a freely available minor leaguer or an AAAA player from his bench, how much value would the team be losing?"

Here's one example: When Yankees catcher Gáry Sanchez was called up from Triple-A on Aug. 3, 2016, the then twenty-three-year old catcher batted .299 with twenty home runs and threw out 41 percent of attempted base stealers in fifty-three games. That accumulated a WAR of 3.0, meaning that Gary Sanchez was worth three wins to the New York Yankees over a freely available minor leaguer or AAA player from their bench. But Gary Sanchez was himself a freely available minor leaguer at the time of his call-up, so are we saying Sanchez was three wins better than himself?

It's not at all uncommon for a player to get called up from the minors and post a higher WAR than a regular position player on his team. But by that definition, that's impossible.

New York Yankees catcher Gary Sanchez, pictured here as a member of the Double-A Trenton Thunder, produced immediately after getting his call to the majors.

## NOTABLE PLAYERS LAST TEN SEASONS CALLED UP AFTER JUNE 1 WITH HIGHER WAR THAN INCUMBENT

|  | Year | WAR | Opening Day Starter (WAR) |
|---|---|---|---|
| Giancarlo Stanton (FLA) | 2009 | 2.8 | Cody Ross (1.6) |
| Manny Machado (BAL) | 2012 | 1.6 | Mark Reynolds (1.2) |
| Francisco Lindor (CLE) | 2015 | 4.6 | José Ramírez (1.4) |
| Carlos Correa (HOU) | 2015 | 4.3 | Jed Lowrie (1.1) |

*WAR—According to Baseball-Reference.com*

Now those four players above are perennial all-stars, and Stanton was named the MVP of the National League in 2017. But how about other players? There have been many notable players who have been called up, sent down, and called back up again, so they are really replacing themselves in a sense.

## NOTABLE PLAYERS LAST 3 SEASONS— SENT DOWN AND CALLED UP

|  | Year | WAR | Transactions |
|---|---|---|---|
| Jackie Bradley Jr. (BOS) | 2015 | 2.2 | Sent down four times |
| Byron Buxton (MIN) | 2016 | 1.8 | Sent down on 8/7, recalled on 9/1 |
| Keon Broxton (MIL) | 2018 | 1.4 | Sent down three times |

*WAR—According to Baseball-Reference.com*

•   •   •

Even a player like Eric Thames, who went to Korea for a few seasons, came back and posted a WAR of 1.4. Maybe it's the definition of the statistic that needs to be changed, but do not tell me that it's judged by a player's replacement level over a minor leaguer when a lot of times we have seen contradictions to that fact.

Another issue with WAR is that there isn't any consistency from source to source. The way Baseball-Reference.com calculates the statistic is different than the way FanGraphs.com calculates it, as you can see below for the same players in the same seasons.

## NOTABLE PLAYERS LAST TEN SEASONS CALLED UP AFTER JUNE 1 WITH HIGHER WAR THAN INCUMBENT

|  | Year | WAR | Opening Day Starter (WAR) |
|---|---|---|---|
| Giancarlo Stanton (FLA) | 2009 | 2.7 | Cody Ross (N/A) |
| Manny Machado (BAL) | 2012 | 1.2 | Mark Reynolds (0.6) |
| Francisco Lindor (CLE) | 2015 | 4.0 | José Ramírez (0.5) |
| Carlos Correa (HOU) | 2015 | 3.4 | Jed Lowrie (1.1) |

*WAR—According to Fangraphs.com*

With the exception of Jed Lowrie and Cody Ross (Fangraphs does not calculate split-season WAR) all the numbers are different. We have questioned all kinds of the standard statistics from wins to batting average to saves, but WAR—a metric that some of the analytical world lives by—is calculated differently by different websites, and yet somehow it's still accepted by the majority in the game even though it isn't recognized by the official stats-keeper of Major League Baseball, the Elias Sports Bureau. It has now become routine to state "bWAR" when referring to

WAR calculated by Baseball-Reference and "fWAR" when referring to WAR calculated by FanGraphs. If two different websites calculated batting average differently the sabermetric world would lose it.

The third thing that's wrong with WAR is how it overvalues defense. We saw this firsthand during the 2015–16 offseason when Jason Heyward was the prized player on the free agent market. Age had something to do with it; Heyward was only twenty-six years old, but this list probably had something to do with him being so sought after:

### HIGHEST WAR AMONG NATIONAL LEAGUE POSITION PLAYERS: 2010–2015

|  |  | All-Star App. | Highest MVP Finish |
|---|---|---|---|
| Joey Votto | 35.7 | 4 | 1 (2010) |
| Andrew McCutchen | 35.1 | 5 | 1 (2013) |
| **Jason Heyward** | **29.8** | **1** | **15 (2015)** |
| Buster Posey | 29.4 | 3 | 1 (2012) |
| Ryan Braun | 27.0 | 5 | 1 (2011) |

*WAR: According to Baseball-Reference*

Heyward, a former first-round pick, was in this group because he had won three Gold Gloves in this span, allowing him to be surrounded by perennial all-stars and MVP winners in the category of WAR. Some used it as an indication that—and he had not yet hit his prime—because he was among that elite group of players, Heyward would soon reach his potential. The Cubs then rewarded him with an eight-year, $184 million contract. That might

The Chicago Cubs signed outfielder Jason Heyward to an eight-year,
$184 million contract in 2016, largely as a result of his WAR.

have been the first time analytics influenced a major free agent signing.

Even some of the game's greatest players are affected by WAR. Albert Pujols is not the dominant player he used to be, but he still knows how to do his job. Since he arrived in the big leagues he has been one of the best run-producers this game has ever seen. He's one of only five players to have driven in two thousand or more career runs. But when we take a look at his 2017 season, it pales in comparison to the bar he had set in his earlier days.

With that said, he drove in 101 runs and scored fifty-three runs in 149 games (designated hitter-143, first base-6). While he was older and hobbled with injuries he still managed to produce 154 combined runs in those 149 games played. Since he only played six games at first base, his -1.2 WAR cannot have anything to do with his declining ability to play first base as well as he once did. His 101 RBIs tied for ninth most in the American League. Referencing the definition of WAR as earlier stated, the minor leagues must be full of well-traveled twenty-eight-year-olds on their fifth organization who can drive in a hundred runs in the big leagues. Albert's .241 batting average, twenty-three home runs, and .672 on-base percentage were not very Albert-like numbers, especially at his $26M salary. It's obvious that he didn't drive the ball the way he used to, but I like to look at the fact that he still drove in a hundred runs without being able to drive the ball. RBI guys—and Albert is and has been one of best—have a knack for putting points on the board when given the opportunity. If someone or some group or something tries to put a negative value on him for the 2017 season, it shows a complete lack of understanding and respect for how hard this game is and how hard it is to drive in a hundred runs in a year. Just because some in the new school dismiss the RBI doesn't validate the absurd claim that Albert was one of the worst players in all of baseball that year.

Surefire first-ballot hall of famer Albert Pujols still managed
to drive in one hundred runs despite having a down year in 2017.

The 2018 Boston Red Sox won 108 games in the regular season on their way to winning the World Series. Forty-four players participated in games for the Sox that season, with a combined 56.8 WAR. Shouldn't the combined WAR be closer to 108? If the combined 56.8 is real, the Red Sox needed 51.2 more wins to get to 108. Mookie Betts led the way with 10.9 wins above replacement, so let's say we round that number up to 11. If Mookie would have missed the entire season and been replaced by a readily available Triple-A player, by definition the Boston Red Sox would have won ninety-seven games. This establishes that the replacement player has a value of zero WAR. If the replacement has a zero value, then the WAR of the combined roster of the 2018 Red Sox should be 108. Trying to measure absolutely everything cannot be done, and I may be taking some liberties with the term or definition of this stat, but if it's gonna be thrown out there as a legitimate statistic and a matter-of-fact real thing, it needs at the very least to be in the ballpark.

Assigning a value to a player based on some formula that differs greatly from the statistics and theories the game was built on to evaluate a player is hard to do. This is where I again must draw a line: *There are too many variables in baseball for some of these mathematical formulas.*

It might be hard for some to understand this next thought. In 2014, the Oakland Athletics had the best record in baseball at the Aug. 31 trade deadline. Their record at that point in the season was 63–35, twenty-eight games over the .500 mark. Yoenis Céspedes was a big part of this Oakland A's team, but an attempt to go out and get a difference-maker for the postseason, the A's traded Cespedes to the Red Sox for Jon Lester and Jonny Gomes. I'm not mad at the A's; I look at this as a move for Oakland to have a guy in Lester who could pitch games one and five in a five-game series or perhaps games one, four, and seven in a seven-games series. Having a number one pitcher to go to has been a formula for World Series teams in the past. At the time of trade Jon Lester was 10–7 with a 2.52 ERA and was looked at as being that number one starter. Now, here's where the value of

Cespedes might have been overlooked. The Oakland A's went 25–39 without Cespedes in their lineup after the trade, fourteen games under .500. In a nutshell, that's a forty-two-game swing. I realize one player does not make a team, but when something like this comes along and smacks you upside your head, it's hard to ignore. The A's finished in second place in the American League West by ten games, clinched a wild-card spot, but lost an epic game to the Royals as Kansas City made their way toward a World Series matchup with the Giants. In baseball, and especially referring to lineup construction in this case, there is something very real about presence. I believe in 2014 with regard to Cespedes and the A's, his missing presence down the stretch was enormous. Other factors may have contributed to the A's decline, and there are some things in baseball that can't be explained, but if it looks like a duck, it probably is.

If I were to try and look at this situation through an analytical lens, a possible argument for Oakland making this trade would have been that trading a 2.9 WAR player in Cespedes for a 2.8 WAR player in Lester came out to a virtual push. And for the A's a push looked like a win. They were in first place and likely figured they'd remain there since they weren't really giving up that much in the trade and were getting back the same value with the possibility of having a horse they could ride through the postseason, as Lester had done for the Red Sox in 2007 and 2013.

I know that this isn't the rationale behind this very questionable statistical definition, but if the shoe fits one should wear it. In theory the trade made sense. In all of the nonmeasurable, presence-of-a-player categories, it obviously didn't work out as planned. If our game's future deals are based on formulas and values without taking into consideration the nonmeasurable components of the players themselves, something important might get overlooked.

The Oakland Athletics missed the presence of Yoenis Cespedes, pictured here as a member of the New York Mets, after they traded him to the Boston Red Sox in 2014.

I'm seeing the sabermetric community sometimes shorten *wins above replacement* to *wins* when referring to a player now. Is this because saying "John Doe is a four-win player" sounds better than "John Doe has a WAR of four"? It does sound cleaner; I'll give them that. But I believe it gets shortened because they know the *above replacement* part of this stat needs help. By shortening the phrase and making it a little catchier, they hope it might just flow by. In either case, the very thought of one number trying to define a player isn't working for me.

If this doesn't work for me now, in the present, I'm sure you know how I feel about going back through time with attempts to adjust, create, or weight numbers in an effort to mathematically determine who is or was the greatest player of all time. Babe Ruth's career WAR is 182.4, while Albert Pujols has the highest career WAR among active players with 100.5. That disparity is extreme considering Pujols' productivity, but the beauty of sport is the debate. If we cannot put an accurate, definitive number on the current players using these formulas, how can we expect to go back through baseball history and get those right? So now we have questionable current numbers being compared to questionable past numbers with the goal of ranking the best of the all-time players. Debates work, but trying to end the debate with "his WAR puts him here" does not.

# CHAPTER 10

# DEFENSIVE RUNS SAVED (DRS)

**D**efensive Runs Saved (or DRS) is another one of the new statistics that I have a hard time buying into. The name of this stat is as misleading as it can possibly be. It does not relate to actually saving runs. The way I understand it, there are formulas in place for plays that are made and plays that are not made. There are different formulas for different defensive positions played. This makes sense because certainly a second baseman can't compare to a leftfielder; but are these different formulas weighted properly? This is where one of my problems lies. Can an outfielder actually be a more valuable defender than any infielder? I think not, but the DRS statistic points to the idea that they can be. This goes against any real baseball common sense. The total chances alone should dismiss any thought of an outfielder's defensive importance over an infielder's.

•　　•　　•

## 2018 MLB DEFENSIVE RUNS SAVED LEADERS

| Among Outfielders | DRS | Total Chances |
|---|---|---|
| JaCoby Jones | 21 | 293 |
| Lorenzo Cain | 20 | 321 |
| Mookie Betts | 20 | 278 |
| Harrison Bader | 19 | 268 |
| Ender Inciarte | 19 | 391 |

| Among Infielders | DRS | Total Chances |
|---|---|---|
| 3B Matt Chapman | 29 | 484 |
| SS Andrelton Simmons | 21 | 610 |
| SS Nick Ahmed | 21 | 606 |
| 2B D.J. LeMahieu | 18 | 591 |
| SS Francisco Lindor | 14 | 586 |
| 1B Matt Olson | 14 | 1,494 |
| C Mike Zunino | 12 | 925 |

In the current weighting system of DRS, clearly the catcher and first baseman get no respect. How can the two players who handle the baseball more than anyone on the field be valued so little defensively? To quote Christopher "Mad Dog" Russo, "Watch the game!" Really, if you truly watch the game you will see five, ten, fifteen balls a night thrown in the dirt by the pitcher when there are two strikes on the hitter or with men on base. Every one of these pitches that comes up short has the chance of resulting in someone picking up ninety feet on the bases. If these pitches happen with a man on third, ninety feet means a run. There's an average of three hundred pitches (150 per team) thrown every night in a big league game. Not all of these pitches get to the catcher, but he has to be ready for every one of them. A catcher might also make a couple of back-door pick-off attempts to first base, maybe keeping that runner a little more honest and in turn preventing him from going first to third on a base hit. It can also allow for a double play to be turned more easily, as the runner on first doesn't get as big of a secondary lead. These two things can't be measured, so I'm sure things like this don't factor into the DRS frame of mind. But just because something can't be measured doesn't mean it isn't real.

The first baseman has the most total chances, which means he is involved in more outs than anyone else on the diamond. My baseball experiences tell me that every defender's participation in recording outs probably falls in the 80 percent "routine" category, meaning four out of five plays are somewhat routine. I believe this holds true for first baseman as well. Some first basemen have taken the ball in the dirt and have made "picking" their own art form. Because these guys make it look so easy, it gets overlooked by some, if not most, observers. Just because it looks easy doesn't mean you should confuse this play for routine. Quite a few highlight-reel plays made by other infielders end with a ball being picked out of the dirt by the first baseman, yet most of, if not all of, the praise goes to the infielder who makes the first half of the play. I value defense at every position, and I also know when defense is not being valued in the way that it should be.

The concept of this new stat is worthy, but as I have said before it's misleading. It was also rushed to market because a select group wanted to show a better way to evaluate defense. The analytics group's belief that *errors* are one of the more outdated and irrelevant statistics was probably the genesis for defensive runs saved. Errors have their own chapter in this book, as they certainly tell a story, and the teams that simply get the outs they are supposed to get without committing errors win games. The early form of DRS was UZR (Ultimate Zone Rating), which broke onto

Matt Chapman of the Oakland Athletics captured the
American League Gold Glove at third base in 2018 and 2019.

the scene some years back, was also rushed to market so it was very flawed and has since become an almost extinct term. UZR will not get its own chapter in this book.

Another one of my big problems is the glaring, head-scratching implications the DRS statistic brings with it. If we attach a DRS number to all players in the game and those numbers indicate that one player is five times the defender that another is, it needs to be examined.

Oakland A's third baseman Matt Chapman has made that point for us after being credited with twenty-nine defensive runs saved in 2018 despite making twenty errors. Nolan Arenado on the other hand, who has won the National League Gold Glove Award for third basemen six seasons in a row, had only six defensive runs saved during that same season. Putting the Gold Glove aside, I know from watching Nolan Arenado play third base that he is one of the game's best defenders. Matt Chapman had a great defensive 2018, I agree, but the 29–6 disparity in DRS says that Chapman is five times the defender than Arenado. Which he isn't.

To take this one step further, a defender in the "negative" for DRS, who clearly is not a subpar defender, is an even bigger cause for concern. Astros all-star third baseman Alex Bregman was listed in 2018 as a -6 DRS and -3 DRS in 2017. Did anyone watch the 2017 Houston Astros postseason run? The defensive display that Bregman put on during that run screams that he's not a *negative* defender. An average or less-than-average third baseman does not make the kinds of plays I saw Bregman make during the Astros run. I fully understand that three playoff series is not representative of a full season, but I also fully understand that when you make plays like the ones Bregman made, there is no way you should have a negative rating in any statistical fielding category.

• • •

Alex Bregman of the Houston Astros was listed as a -6 DRS in 2018, but the fielder I saw made all the plays he had to make.

If these two areas of concern have question marks this big, how can we be sure of anything else DRS has to offer?

If these numbers aren't really reflective of reality, then we need a better way of putting these numbers out there. It seems that any time these numbers are being used in a broadcast or studio show, they get thrown out in a blanket statement, such as "He led all of baseball in defensive runs saved." If we use that blanket statement, we are simply not telling any truth relative to actual baseball common sense. If we say a hitter led all of baseball with a .342 batting average, this is a *fact* that means something. If we do the same regarding DRS, it doesn't really mean anything because it doesn't relate to a real number. To me, DRS is a concept that needs to go back to the drawing board. Derek Jeter won five Gold Gloves at shortstop and made all the plays he had to make for the Yankees, yet sabermetricians would have you believe his -152 DRS between 2003 and the end of his career made him one of the worst defenders of his era. That's absurd.

The DRS police may (I said may) get the best defensive players at each position right. But the system of trying to put a number of defensive runs saved to a player or position simply isn't working. A shortstop could have five possible chances in a game, with four of them being "above average" in nature, and he could handle them all and record the outs. All four of these plays could happen with no one on base. His fifth chance might come when there are runners on second and third with two outs. It could be a routine two-hopper that he catches and throws high over the first baseman's head, allowing two runs scored.

If the DRS formula wasn't locked away in a vault, I would be able to tell you that what I'm about to say is 100 percent accurate, but since it is locked away, I'm going to have to speculate. The five chances this shortstop had to make plays on this day could have garnered him an uptick on his DRS. The two runs that scored are irrelevant to the creators and users of the DRS stat. Actual runs don't matter. If this is true, and I believe it to be, how can we let this statistic carry any weight at all?

Block Man was introduced on Bill's BlackBoard to stress the importance of catchers being able to block balls in the dirt and keep runners at bay.

# CHAPTER 11

# OVERSHIFTS AND DEFENSIVE POSITIONING

The New York Yankees opened their 2012 season on the road against the Tampa Bay Rays. Tampa finished six games behind the Yanks in 2011 and has been a thorn in the Yankees' backside since Joe Maddon took over as manager in 2006. The Yankees left St. Petersburg with an 0–3 record and even more frustration with their division rivals. Game after game, day after day, left-handed Yankee hitters such as Mark Teixeira, Robinson Canó, Curtis Granderson, and Nick Swisher all came back to the dugout flummoxed. Why? Because ground balls that they thought would be hits were now outs.

**NEW YORK YANKEES NOTABLE LEFT-HANDED HITTERS VS. RAYS: APRIL 6–8, 2012**

|  | H-AB | Ground Balls | GIDP |
|---|---|---|---|
| Robinson Canó | 3–13 | 8 | 1 |
| Mark Teixeira | 1–9 | 2 | 0 |

| | H-AB | Ground Balls | GIDP |
|---|---|---|---|
| Curtis Granderson | 2–12 | 5 | 1 |
| Nick Swisher | 3–11 | 3 | 0 |
| **Combined** | **9–45** | **18** | **2** |

This helped to usher in the popularity of the overshift. The overshift became a part of many team's daily game day defensive alignments. It seemed that when any left-handed power hitter stepped up to home plate it was an automatic that the shortstop moved to the second base side of the infield, the third baseman slid over and basically took the shortstop's place, and the second baseman backed up into short right field. From then to now, different organizations have tweaked which players play where in the basic overshift configuration, but their goal is the same: to limit the amount of space a left-handed pull hitter has to get a ball past the infield. When left-handed power hitters come to the dish, some teams have taken the third baseman and pushed him out into short right field to keep the second baseman and short stop closer to their comfort zones. In the beginning phase of the overshifts, they were mostly being employed when there was no one on base. I believe defensive positioning should revert back to more of that way of thinking.

It's important to remember that like many of the things we've been discussing in this book, defensive shifts are nothing new. The great Ted Williams of the Boston Red Sox famously faced overshifts for a significant portion of his career, even in the year he hit .406, and shifts are known to have been employed as far back as the 1920s. I recall standing in short right field in the Metrodome in Minnesota when Kent Hrbek came to the plate with nobody on base. The Orioles teams I played on also employed shifts against Steve Balboni, a dead pull hitter, in his days with the Yankees.

The great Ted Williams of the Boston Red Sox famously faced
overshifts for a significant portion of his career, including the year he hit .406.

### Did Joe Maddon Stick with the Overshift?

The example we used at the beginning was Joe Maddon and the
Tampa Bay Rays, who may have been at the forefront of this
revolution and led all of baseball at the time. But later on when
the Cubs—under Joe's leadership—had the second fewest overshifts in all of baseball, they broke the curse of the goat and won
the 2016 World Series. Everyone else in baseball has been increas-
ing the number of shifts, but when Joe joined the Cubs he went
in the opposite direction.

## MOST SHIFTS FROM 2012–2014

| | |
|---|---|
| **Tampa Bay Rays** | **2,873** |
| Houston Astros | 2,577 |
| Baltimore Orioles | 2,373 |
| Toronto Blue Jays | 2,113 |
| New York Yankees | 2,081 |

## FEWEST SHIFTS—2016

| | |
|---|---|
| Miami Marlins | 97 |
| **Chicago Cubs** | **262** |
| Kansas City Royals | 335 |
| San Francisco Giants | 342 |
| New York Mets | 459 |

The 2016 Cubs had four pitchers who started thirty-plus games and a fifth guy who made twenty-nine starts. This type of consistency can also play into the idea of how much we need to overshift. I wonder if the teams that do more of the shifting believe they have the pitching to get hitters out. If I ran a team and believed that my pitchers were going to give up rockets, I may need to have three guys on the pull side of the infield. But if I believe my pitchers can make a pitch and jam someone, inducing weak contact, two guys on a side would work just fine.

We've seen the number of overshifts multiply since their early day use. When at first the use of the overshift was limited to a couple of left-handed power hitters with no one on base, it is now common for four, five, maybe even six hitters (left-handed or right-handed) in any given lineup to face an overshift during a game, with bases empty or with runners on base. The overshift wasn't invented by the new school. But the overshift "gone crazy" is a creation of the new way of thinking about the game.

Joe Maddon, pictured here as the manager of the Chicago Cubs, is believed to have ushered in the newfound popularity of the defensive overshift.

Let's take a closer look with some numbers. There's a lot to look at and it can be a bit confusing, so I'll give a brief introduction to the table below. The difference between the numbers produced by Inside Edge and Fan Graphs is simple; Inside Edge includes "extreme shades" as an overshift. An extreme shade is when two defenders are still positioned on each side of the infield, but either the shortstop or the second baseman are very close to being directly behind the second-base bag. The AVG column represents overall league-wide batting average. The AVG in Shift represents players' batting averages when the shift is on and BABIP represents the league-wide batting average when the ball is put into play.

| | MLB OVER SHIFTS SINCE 2012 | | | | |
|---|---|---|---|---|---|
| | Inside Edge | Fan Graphs | AVG | AVG in Shift | *BABIP |
| 2012 | 12,167 | 4,550 | .255 | .275 | .297 |
| 2013 | 9,836 | 6,851 | .253 | .257 | .297 |
| 2014 | 19,014 | 7,691 | .251 | .282 | .299 |
| 2015 | 21,322 | 13,222 | .254 | .288 | .299 |
| 2016 | 34,533 | 17,633 | .255 | .285 | .300 |
| 2017 | 27,778 | 26,561 | .255 | .279 | .300 |
| 2018 | 36,633 | 27,924 | .248 | .276 | .296 |

If I'm reading these numbers correctly, 2013 looks like it was the best year for the overshift, and with that said I'm not sure what else can actually point to the overshift working at all except, perhaps, situationally.

There are three scenarios to consider when discussing the full-blown overshift.

1. **It doesn't matter:** A ball is hit to the right side of the infield by a big, left-handed power hitter. The play-by-play guy will say, "He hit it right into the shift." That is a fact, but in most cases these ground balls are not squared up and would have been an out if there were just two guys

on that side of the infield. Even so, those outs are now perceived to be a direct result of the overshift.

2. **Take a hit away:** A rocket is hit by the same left-handed hitter that would split the first and second baseman in normal, straight-up positioning, but because of the overshift the second baseman is now located in that hole in short right field and is able to make the play. "That's been a hit for a hundred years," a broadcaster might say, "but not anymore because of the smart positioning in today's game."

3. **Give a hit:** Once again that same left-handed hitter cues one off the end of the bat and the ball rolls straight away toward third base, but because of the overshift the third baseman is basically playing shortstop. The commentary here usually resembles that of crickets.

According to Inside Edge and these three categories, the overshift works 1 percent of the time. A few thoughts come to mind when I see numbers like these. If 1 percent is the average of all thirty teams using the overshift, does that mean that fifteen teams are slightly above the mark and fifteen teams are slightly below the mark? Or is it that ten teams do it really well while the other twenty teams are just bad at defensive alignments? If all teams use the overshift and it really works, that 1 percent would have to be higher, wouldn't it? These teams must have their own numbers regarding the effectiveness of shifts.

•  •  •

# THE OVERSHIFT HAS HURT CERTAIN PLAYERS OVER THE PAST FEW YEARS

Most of these guys who have lost hits as a result of the shift are the ones for whom the overshift was originally designed: left-handed power hitters. I believe the biggest part of the effectiveness in neutralizing some of these players is mental. Losing a few hits to the shift can climb into a hitter's dome, unless you're Ted Williams.

This has resulted in a "Why put the ball in play if it's gonna be an out anyway?" approach. If it's truly a home run or strikeout mentality and the power numbers are still there, I can live with having one of these guys in my lineup, but if home runs and average decline and strikeouts keep going up, that player becomes less useful to me.

There are left-handed power hitters in the game who have not been affected by these overshifts in any sort of meaningful way. They've been able to maintain their batting averages and homers by making the necessary adjustments when facing these defensive alignments. In my opinion, the conversation around banning such defensive positioning is off base for sure. The number of players truly affected by these shifts is very few. If these players cannot or are not willing to make any adjustments, the blame should be placed squarely on them. Those in the game have been talking more and more about getting more versatile athletes in the sport. If the overshift weeds out a few one-dimensional players, that might not be such a bad thing.

The Cubs' Anthony Rizzo is a left-handed power hitter who has survived the shift. He still might be a pull hitter and have the overshift thrown at him from time to time, but he has found a way to maintain his numbers.

| HIGHEST BATTING AVERAGE VS. SHIFT FROM 2016–2018—MIN. 700 OPPORTUNITIES | | |
| --- | --- | --- |
| | AVG vs. Shift | Career AVG through 2018 |
| Freddie Freeman | .335 | .293 |
| Cody Bellinger | .308 | .263 |
| Carlos González | .302 | .287 |
| Matt Carpenter | .292 | .274 |
| **Anthony Rizzo** | **.282** | **.270** |

Once again if I'm reading these numbers correctly, all five guys hit better than their career average when the overshift is used against them. Seven hundred opportunities is basically equivalent to one full season. Each one of these hitters probably wishes all teams would overshift them all year, every year.

In the old school days we would have a pitchers meeting on the first day of a series and go over the opposing hitters. During this meeting we would go over various spray charts, look at the reports of the advanced scout who just watched our opponent play in their prior series, and draw upon our personal experience to come up with game plans for our pitching staff and our defensive alignments. During my first five-and-a-half years in the big leagues, I was able to watch and learn from one of the game's best in my big brother, Cal Jr. He was the captain for sure, but there was no real need for a big C on his chest. His knowledge and recollection of hitters' tendencies were unmatched. He took the lead as far as our infield positioning went most of the time; it was a combination of how we would pitch certain hitters and their tendencies. If we executed the game plan right, the defense usually found itself in the right place. If you game-planned a certain left-handed hitter with a "Pitch him away, play him away" approach, which was fairly common back in the day, and the pitcher decided to trick him by throwing something inside, the defensive players looked as if they were in the wrong place.

As the shortstop and as our most experienced infielder, if Jr. moved a step toward the pull side with a right-handed hitter in the box facing a 2–0 count, he'd give me a quick shout and hold up one finger, and I'd give him one to two steps up the middle and pull the first baseman with me. He would also push the third baseman one step closer to the line.

We tried to work as a defensive unit, and if the pitcher as the front line of that unit executed the pitch properly, things could go really well. Jr. led the league many times in assists, putouts, and total chances. Granted, he played 162 games every year, which didn't hurt. He was also characterized as oversized and slow of foot for a shortstop. How could a shortstop who was too big and slow lead the league in these categories? I like to think one reason was that he was in the right spot a lot. I also know that his anticipation and first step was on point. He, and therefore we, would regularly play a hitter in three or four spots during the course of an at-bat depending on who was pitching and what the count was. Knowing which hitters would change their thought processes during an at-bat based on whether the count was in their favor or not was key.

I do believe that more hitters in today's game have one single approach compared to hitters back in the day, and that approach doesn't vary with the count at all. It is an all-or-nothing jog around the bases or a slow walk back to the dugout. I also believe some of the new thoughts involving hitters' spray charts don't cater to who's pitching, the count, or the game situation. It simply tells where the hitter hits the ball. These two things have led to the cheat sheets defensive players keep in their back pockets and under their hats. I'm coming to the sad conclusion that the thinking part of defensive baseball is going by the wayside. Instincts are being squashed. If you think something or say something formed by your own observations, you have a chance to learn and retain something. But if all you do is follow a script, the learning stagnates. I'm beginning to see the inclusion of robots playing defense by looking at a computer-generated print out of where to stand on the field hitter by hitter. I don't believe this holds true for all teams, though. I still believe the better defensive players and better defensive teams use the positioning printouts as a guide but also rely on their instincts and experience as the game unfolds, watching how the pitcher is attacking hitters and reading the hitters' swings.

Let's take a look at Game 5 of the 2015 National League division series between the Mets and Dodgers. The Mets won the game 3–2 and won the series, eventually going onto the World Series, where they lost to the Royals. Zack Greinke was the starting pitcher for the Dodgers on this night and his line was 6.2 IP, 6 H, 1 BB, 9 K, 3 ER. I would and will argue that this line score should have been better. Two of these three runs allowed were a direct result of an overshifting Dodger defense. If someone wants to argue that Greinke's 2015 success was a result of all the overshifts played behind him they can have at it, but I'm not buying it. I know enough to say that when Zack Greinke took the mound in 2015, the Dodgers could have played defense in the alignment Abner Doubleday laid out in the game's early days and he still would have been just fine. Greinke had a record of 19–3 with a 1.66 ERA during the 2015 season and had already won game two of this series, giving up only two solo home runs in seven innings of work. Yes, those two home runs and one more home run in Game 5 were *solo*; does any pitcher want to give up big flies? No, but the good ones seem to give them up when there's no one on base, if and when they do give them up. So let's get back to my cherry picking of this one game, sample size be damned.

Zack Greinke, pictured here as a member of the Arizona Diamondbacks, was
victimized by defensive overshifts in a 2015 playoff game versus the New York Mets.

In the top of the first inning, the Mets' Curtis Granderson reached first base on an infield knock on a weak ground ball toward the second base area. Howie Kendrick (2B) was in short right field, while Justin Turner (3B) was on the second base side of second base and shading the middle of the infield. Turner fielded this slow roller, but the throw to first was not in time. With one out now, Daniel Murphy hit a left centerfield gapper that scored Granderson. Greinke then stranded Murphy with a couple of punch outs to limit the damage to that one run, but Granderson shouldn't have been on base with a chance to score in the first place.

In the top of the fourth and with Murphy on first with one out, Lucas Duda worked a walk. Greinke had some favorable matchups after Duda, but Murphy astutely ran to second base and then broke for third without a play because nobody was covering the base during the overshift on Duda. Was the Dodger infield taking a nap during that walk? Probably, but a more conventional defense would have allowed for that nap without any extra bases being taken. Travis d'Arnaud then delivered a sacrifice fly, scoring Murphy, and the Mets tied the score 2–2. Greinke did later give up the winning run on a solo shot to Murphy, who was red hot that postseason, in the top of sixth, and the Dodgers weren't able to score in the final four innings. They ended up losing 3–2, but in my opinion, two of the three runs scored by the Mets in that critical game could have been prevented simply by playing straight up defense. Is this cherry picking? I guess so, but it's a big fat cherry that's extremely ripe for the picking. There are all kinds of examples of one-game sample sizes over the baseball seasons, and when you start adding them up, patterns begin to emerge. The overall batting average against Greinke was .187 during this incredible year but during the 11.2 percent of the time that the overshift was played behind him, batters hit at a .315 clip. Needless to say, pitchers who can pitch should have more say in how the defense is positioned behind them.

In today's game we see more and more players looking at cheat sheets for defensive positioning. If a defensive player is truly being told where to play on every hitter and then that defensive player receives a negative or subpar DRS rating, shouldn't some of that rating belong to whoever created that index card in the player's back pocket or hat? From the previous chapter, you know I don't think Alex Bregman is a subpar defender, yet in the 2017 and 2018 seasons he was listed as a combined -8 DRS. By the time of the 2019 All-Star Game he was listed at a +5 DRS. Should I take this to mean that over the offseason he put in extra work on the defensive side of the ball? Or did the Houston Astros tweak their already aggressive forms of defensive positioning? I find it hard to believe that Bregman all of the sudden just got better at playing third base when I know he was already pretty good to begin with. My point is that some players might receive a bad defensive rating simply because they're not being put in the right position to make the play.

# CHAPTER 12

# ERRORS

I f something in the game is considered outdated, there should be something better to replace it. When it comes to the new defensive metrics, however, this is not the case. The attempts at finding a better way to value a defender have included Ultimate Zone Rating (UZR), Defensive Runs Saved (DRS), Defensive Wins Above Replacement (DWAR), and Outs Above Average (OAA). All of these involve complicated formulas, and even the users of these new defensive stats admit that they're not perfect. But if these new defensive metrics aren't perfect, what's the rush to replace errors?

I have access to an incredible research staff at MLB Network. I can be on the desk doing one of our nightly shows and see good and bad defensive plays being made all night long. If a certain player interests me one way or another, I can ask one of my researchers to tell me how today's plays affected that player's DRS. The answer I'll get back from my researcher would be "I don't know." That's because the information isn't available; it is kept behind closed doors with even the MLB Network researchers kept in the dark regarding how it's calculated. Yet at the end of the baseball season, all the defenders get a magic number assigned to them. Those numbers become public, and one player ends up leading all of baseball in defensive runs saved. How can this be?

The reason the new defensive metrics have holes in them is because judging a defensive player or team isn't an exact science. The situations are fluid, yet it seems as if those creating these statistics quite simply don't understand that. The game inside the game cannot be measured by a spreadsheet, but it can be measured by a qualified, crusty baseball man. If the new school movement truly wants all the information that can be ascertained, the crusty baseball man is necessary.

When it comes to talking defense, the way to determine if a player or a team is good or not is to watch them. I would trust an old schooler to follow a squad for three months and watch them play. At the end of the three months, I could get a detailed report from what he has seen. This report would cover all of the individual, everyday players and the overall team's defensive capabilities. It would also cover game situations, common sense, and the extent to which certain players "just don't get it." The added bonus in having experienced human eyes watching the one team play is the reports on every opposing player and team his scouted team played. This type of scouting and the information that can be acquired from it are priceless.

Are the errors and fielding percentage statistics perfect? No. The official scorer is usually an old, local newspaper writer, but I still believe that these stats are a fairly accurate reflection of which players are better defenders and therefore which teams are better defensively than others are. If you make fewer errors than the other team does, you'll win 60 percent of the time. Generally speaking, a team that makes fewer errors than other teams do have good defensive players, and I believe they also pay attention to detail a bit more than a squad that commits a lot of errors. Bad team defense tends to have a domino effect. Routine errors lead to players throwing to the wrong base, pitchers not backing up bases, cutoff men being in the wrong spot or being overthrown, wild pitches, and passed balls. A team that makes a lot of errors has this kind of stuff going on more than a team that makes fewer errors does. The team that commits fewer physical routine errors has discipline in the way the game should be played defensively. With every ball put into play by the hitter, a defender should be on the move. This applies whether it's a two-hopper right at the shortstop with no one on base or it's a line drive toward the left centerfield gap with the bases loaded. Individual defenders make up the overall team defense. The more the individuals master the routine, the better the overall team defense will be.

### WINNING PERCENTAGE OF TEAMS WITH FEWER ERRORS THAN OPPONENT SINCE 2012

| | |
|---|---|
| 2012 | .614 |
| 2013 | .637 |
| 2014 | .622 |
| 2015 | .636 |
| 2016 | .609 |
| 2017 | .644 |
| 2018 | .615 |
| **Overall** | **.625** |

These winning percentages, over 162 games, put that team in the playoffs every time.

For the most part, I do believe that the definitions in the official rulebook of Major League Baseball for what constitutes a hit or an error are accurate:

**Hit:** A hit occurs when a batter strikes the baseball into fair territory and reaches base without doing so via an error or a fielder's choice. There are four types of hits in baseball: singles, doubles, triples, and home runs. All four are counted equally when deciphering batting average. If a player is thrown out attempting to take an extra base (e.g., turning a single into a double), that still counts as a hit.

**Error:** A fielder is given an error if, in the judgment of the official scorer, he fails to convert an out on a play that an average fielder should have made. Fielders can also be given errors if they make a poor play that allows one or more runners to advance on the bases. A batter does not necessarily need to reach base for a fielder to be given an error. If he drops a foul ball that extends an at-bat, that fielder can also be assessed an error.

Does the official scorekeeper in the press box of every big league stadium get every decision right when determining what's a hit and what's an error? No, and this is one of the biggest complaints by some in the new school community. A person in the press box making questionable scoring decisions is a problem for the people who have come up with complicated formulas to determine a player's defensive value. The errors or hits given out on questionable plays, "sun balls," and "I got it, you take it" balls are at a minimum compared to cut-and-dry hits or errors. Even the scoring decisions that could go either way aren't all that frequent, and those have a way of evening out over the long haul.

I'm not saying that two wrongs make a right, but I am saying that if two shortstops are separated by ten errors by the year's end, the one with more errors likely was not the victim of poor scorekeeping. Over the full baseball season, both players probably had about the same number of questionable scoring decisions made against them. While "hometown" scorers do exist, things tend to come out in the wash over the course of 162 games.

If we as an industry are truly getting smarter with all the information at our disposal that allows us to better predict where hitters will hit the ball, why wouldn't we care about the ball hit right at us? Most everyone who has ever played the game has made a great play, but very few can catch a ball hit right at them and then throw the ball on the money to record an out ninety-nine times out of a hundred. An infielder's range or ability to get to ground balls hit to his right or left is valuable if an out is recorded. It is also valuable if there's a runner on second base and getting to the ball prevents a run, even if an out isn't recorded. Historically, some infielders with "good range" have made more errors than have guys with "average range," and the supporters of these bigger range guys with more errors like to say, "He gets to more balls." I will address this statement with two questions:

Does he?

*If* he does and then he boots them, what good is that?

In the late '80s and early '90s before the shortstop boom of Derek Jeter, Alex Rodriguez, and Nomar Garciaparra, my brother was the only true "big" shortstop in the game. Whenever Jr. was compared to smaller guys in the American League, like Ozzie Guillén and Tony Fernández, the words "good range" were usually applied to those two, which would make you think that they got to more balls than Jr. did. But in his first ten years in the big leagues, Jr. was nearly on the top of the list of total chances, putouts, and assists.

## CAL RIPKEN JR.

- 5 Times Led AL in Total Chances (1983–1984, 1989, 1991, 1993)
- 6 Times Led AL in Putouts (1984–1985, 1988–1989, 1991, 1993)
- 7 Times Led AL in Assists (1983–1984, 1986–1987, 1989, 1991, 1993)

Give me four infielders with average range who can make all the plays they are supposed to make and I'm golden. The next game you watch closely, count how many far-ranging plays are made by the infielders compared to the number of routine plays made. The routine plays will outweigh the far-ranging plays. Watching a shortstop go deep into the hole, catch a ground ball, get off a strong throw, and get the out at first base is one of my favorite things to watch. Seeing the first part of that play and then watching the throw sail high and wide and the runner ending up on second base is one of my least favorite things to watch.

In the NFL, "Win the turnover battle and win the game" is a motto that has been used for a long time. This is still used and practiced in today's game. Why? Because it still holds true most of the time. In the NBA, a team loses and points out that they turned the ball over too many times. Both situations can be directly compared to baseball. Take care of the ball, no matter what sport, and you'll give your team a better chance to win. In football and basketball, turning the ball over takes away from scoring possibilities while giving your opponent a chance to score. In baseball, making an error or not getting the out that you should have allows another hitter to get to home plate with the chance to do damage. Every hitter who reaches the batter's box because of an error allows your opponent's best hitter to get one step closer to another at-bat himself. Twenty-seven outs are required to win a nine-inning game, while every extra out given to the opposition increases their chances of scoring runs. Getting three outs in an inning is difficult enough sometimes, but making an error on a semi-routine play in one of these types of innings can be a hard thing to overcome.

We should continue trying to come up with a new team error statistic that does address bad defensive plays independent of the official scorekeeper's duties. The hits and errors can continue as is, but we need to put more focus on the team side of defense by looking at missed opportunities to make plays, keeping base runners from advancing, and making bad overall decisions. For now, if a team makes a lot of individual errors, I can assume with a fairly high degree of certainty that overall sloppy defensive play will run rampant over the course of the full season. A few of these teams may reach the playoffs, but the majority of the postseason field will be made up of teams that quite simply take care of the ball.

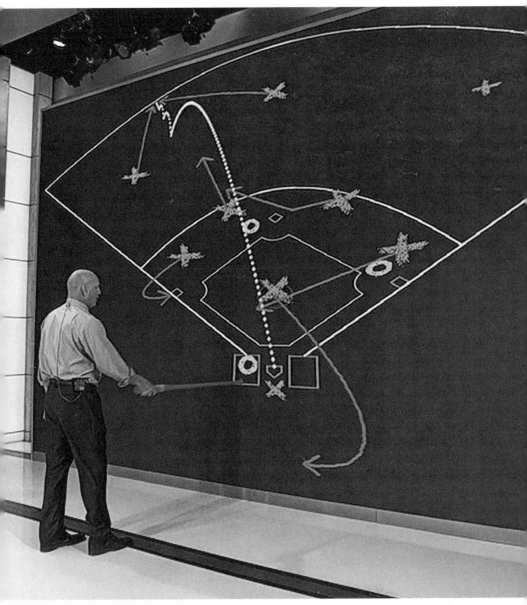

When the ball is put in play, everyone on the defensive side has a responsibility and a job to do. In the next frame the right fielder will be on the move to 2nd base!

# CHAPTER 13

# AUTOMATED STRIKE ZONE AND BALL-STRIKE UMPIRES

The idea of an automated strike zone or "robo-umps" has gained some momentum over the past few years. At first I wanted nothing to do with this idea, but I have softened to it a bit as time has gone on. I'm still not sure that the automated zone can be completely accurate. The front edge of the seventeen-inch-wide home plate is a constant, and the pitcher's release point, whether right-or left-handed, shouldn't be a factor, as the ball crossing the front edge of home plate is the thing that matters. If we were only considering those two things, I would say we have something; however it's fair to say that 6'7" Aaron Judge of the Yankees and 5'6" José Altuve of the Astros have very different strike zones. I would also say that no two hitters in a given lineup have the exact same strike zone. The up and down of my strike zone will be defined as one baseball higher than the belt buckle to the hollow of the knee. The rulebook states that a strike falls between the letters on the jersey to the hollow of the knee. The letters, as far as I can remember, have never been part of a strike zone. My in

It's fair to say that 6'7" Aaron Judge of the Yankees and 5'6"
José Altuve of the Astros have very different strike zones.

and out of the strike is defined as any part of the baseball crossing any part of the front edge of home plate. The up and down and the in and out must overlap. Can we calibrate such an automated strike zone, one that is completely accurate yet changes from hitter to hitter? I don't know the answer, as it is outside my area of expertise. If this can happen without flaw, I may be able to be swayed into adopting such a game-changing adaptation.

The current system of knowing every fourth day that one member of the four-man umpiring crew is going to be behind home plate calling balls and strikes isn't working. If it were working, there would not be any discussion about robo-umps. We have the technology to do a pretty good job of tracking every umpire's performance behind home plate, and yet I'm not sure how we use this information. Since 2009, Major League Baseball has used a zone evaluation system, otherwise known as ZE. ZE grades calls on every pitch not put into play or fouled off based on video from high-speed cameras. Umpires get their report cards the day after the game and can review video for themselves if they wish.

An umpire at first base has the plate the next night. There can be several close plays at first on any given night, and a couple of those calls might get overturned on review. In a case of an overturned call, it simply says, "The umpire was wrong."

## FORCE PLAY REVIEWS FROM 2014–2018

- 2,131 Force Play Reviews at 1B
- 61.8% Overturned (1,318)
- 13.7% Confirmed (293)
- 24.5% Call Stands (520)

• • •

The first base umpire then has to call balls and strikes the next night. Say there's a 1–2 count on the hitter and a close pitch near the outside edge is called strike three on the batter. The hitter protests and the umpire is confident that he didn't miss the pitch. How can the umpire act high and mighty over this pitch when the previous night several of his calls at first base were overturned? These confrontations happen just as described. The things said during these altercations can never be taken back and will be remembered. Sometimes they result in ejections. Trying to eliminate some of these situations can only be beneficial for baseball.

I also question if some of the umpires make adjustments or bear down any harder to try to improve their skills. As far as I know, umpires don't get sent down to AAA. Like the US Supreme Court, it seems that once you get the full-time job as a big league umpire you have that job until you call it quits. This type of setup would allow anyone to have some "just go through the motion" moments, especially down the stretch of a long season. This certainly does not apply to all umpires, but it also undoubtedly hits the mark on some others.

But before we go down the automated road, I'd like to have one last shot at keeping the look of the game the same as we have it today—or at least to keep it a little bit the same. Let's take a look at ball-strike umpires and base umpires. There will always be better performers than others. This certainly holds true in umpiring, especially behind home plate. If we were to have the very best ball-strike umpires working on that full time, can't we make the assumption that they might even get better at what they do? I say yes. I refuse to believe that we can't find umpires that can be in a 93–95 percent accuracy range in calling pitches.

## FIVE HIGHEST CALLED STRIKE PERCENTAGES

**2018 MLB**

| | |
|---|---|
| Ben May | 94.0% |
| John Libka | 94.0% |
| Vic Carapazza | 93.5% |
| Shane Livensparger | 93.4% |
| Will Little | 93.4% |

## FIVE LOWEST CALLED STRIKE PERCENTAGES

**2018 MLB**

| | |
|---|---|
| Rob Drake | 89.4% |
| Joe West | 90.0% |
| Gerry Davis | 90.3% |
| Ed Hickox | 90.3% |
| Laz Díaz | 90.4% |

If we can find forty-five of these umpires, we can put three on every crew. The four-man crew then turns into a five-man crew. The three home plate umpires go on a rotation of home to second to off. In a three-game series, umpire A gets the plate in Game 1; in Game 2 he gets second base. This gives him a great view of every pitch thrown. On day three he should be in a booth watching the game on a monitor. This way he can focus on balls and strikes on all three days. This program would have these guys calling balls and strikes every third night instead of every fourth night. The fourteen or so extra games he'd get behind the dish should necessitate a pay raise for these new ball-strike umpires, which I imagine would appeal to them. The two base umpires would go back and forth between first and third base each night, and this adjustment of their role would be reflected in a pay adjustment in the other direction, collective bargaining be damned.

This system will increase the number of umpires and will put the best umpires behind the plate calling balls and strikes. The less experienced or skilled umpires will only be working the bases and will have the aid of instant replay. Over the last few years, there have been umpires who have proven that they should not be behind the plate because of missing too many pitches and because

I guarantee Sr. and Jr. said some things here
that could not be taken back.

they have reacted inappropriately toward players after they missed one of those pitches.

To keep the automated strike zone out of the game, the umpires are going to have to come around a bit in their thinking. There needs to be a weeding out process and more accountability on their end as well. Umpires will need to perform at a high level to maintain their position in the game.

By the time this book hits the market Major League Baseball will have had about a half a season of a trial run of the automated strike zone in the Atlantic League. The partnership with Major League Baseball and this independent minor league has allowed baseball to experiment with several rule change ideas as well as other initiatives. Since this is a league that isn't tied to any MLB affiliates, it can adopt a variety of rules and can freely experiment with new things. The automated strike zone being used in this league, in which an umpire calls the balls and strikes after a computer tells him if they're balls or strikes, is going to be a conversation moving forward. My gut tells me it will be a work in progress, and I don't believe it will be as good or as bad as the supporters or naysayers will tell you. This means it would likely be a "push" to the current system. I'm not ready for it yet, but if the umpires themselves don't improve and the technology continues to improve, you never know. It seems to work just fine in tennis.

I believe baseball's best bet is to identify the best ball-strike umpires and have them work diligently on their craft. If baseball can't do this and umpires aren't willing to put in the extra work, the robo-ump will someday make his big league debut.

# CHAPTER 14

# RUNS BATTED IN (RBI)

R uns and RBIs are like peanut butter and jelly—they just go together. But just as the analytics community has railed against the importance of batting average, they've done the same with runs batted in. I hate to use the phrase, but "back when I played" the best sluggers in the game drove in a hundred runs. Guys like Eddie Murray, Fred McGriff, Jim Rice, and Juan González were known for always driving in a hundred runs a season; if they didn't, it was considered a down season. Consider some of the best hitters in the game today: Mike Trout, Bryce Harper, Manny Machado, Kris Bryant, and Nolan Arenado. Here's how many hundred-plus RBI seasons they have:

•   •   •

## NUMBER OF 100+ RBI SEASONS AMONG NOTABLE PLAYERS THROUGH THE 2019 SEASON

|  | RBI | Seasons |
| --- | --- | --- |
| Kris Bryant | 1 | 5 |
| Bryce Harper | 2 | 8 |
| Manny Machado | 1 | 8 |
| Mike Trout | 3 | 9 |
| Nolan Arenado | 5 | 7 |

The RBI column used to be the first thing everyone looked at when you looked at a player's stat sheet or baseball card. Now it may be the fifth or sixth thing you look at. I bet if you quizzed a bunch of average baseball fans, not many would know who led the majors in runs batted in last year.

Let's look at a couple of ways players score and drive in runs so we can really examine the statistics runs scored (R) and runs batted in (RBI).

**Solo home run:** The home run hitter gets an R and an RBI in the box score. Neither of these things were dependent on anything except the hitter himself. He hit the ball over the fence, jogged around the bases, crossed home plate, and got credited with a run scored and an RBI.

**Runner on second base–base hit:** The scoring base runner is given a run scored. The hitter who got the base hit is given an RBI. The runner on second base would not have scored if the hitter didn't get a hit, and if there were not a runner on second base, the hitter would not get an RBI for getting that hit. This looks like equal dependency on each other.

Runs are needed to win games; if no one drives in runs, you don't score. The more runs driven in, the more runs you score and the better the chance you have of winning. Unless the runs scored are from a solo home run, a steal of home, an error, or a wild pitch-passed ball, the scoring player is relying on one of his teammates to drive him in.

I'm really not sure why some in the new school recognize runs scored and almost completely dismiss the RBI. The two stats seem like they go hand in hand. The old school recognizes and likes hits, runs, and ribbies. Old school benchmarks should still be the goal of every offensive player: a .300 batting average, a hundred runs scored, a hundred RBIs. Can a player post these numbers and still have had a bad year? I think not. Players who can score a hundred and drive in a hundred are stars of the game without looking at any other numbers, whether real or the so-called normalized. The players who are on top of the leader boards in runs scored put themselves in a position to score runs. The players who challenge for the RBI title do what they need to do to drive runs in when opportunities are presented. Some players quite simply have a knack for driving in runs more than other players do. The home run comes into play in both statistical categories; a thirty–home run guy who hits the old school benchmarks needs to score and drive in seventy more runs. A guy who hits twenty home runs and drives in a hundred runs might have that RBI knack over a guy who hits thirty and drives in ninety. The RBI guy is a foreign concept to some in the new school because they can't measure his makeup. Since they can't measure it, the RBI guy must not be real. This is a little strange to me as this same group takes actual numbers and turns them into something conceptual.

Not everyone can hit these benchmarks. The talent of the player and lineup construction can certainly impact these numbers. Give me a guy or two who can take charge and wants to drive in runs and I will put them in the good old-fashioned three and four spots in my lineup and be just fine.

Weighted Runs Created Plus (wRC+) takes the statistic runs created and adjusts that number to account for important external factors such as ballpark or era. It's adjusted, so a wRC+ of 100 is league average and 150 would be 50 percent above league average.

This newly invented statistic seems to account for runs being important. I question if this is needed in player evaluation, as it seems to say a lot without actually saying anything. *Weighted*, *created*, and *adjusted* are all words that are used when you alter or make up something. *Runs* is the only word in this four-word statistic that actually represents something real; however, by having all the other fabricated words around it, it turns the one real thing into something fictional. Some use this as a predictor of a player's future performance. If I'm looking to acquire a player and look at his last three years and I see .300-100-100, I feel pretty good; provided the player stays healthy, years four, five, and six should look pretty much the same. There are other factors that play into these numbers, but creating, adjusting, and weighting all the old school numbers in an effort to downplay or even get rid of the true numbers of the game seems a little extreme to me, especially when these new measures of a player are not a locked down guarantee of anything.

# CHAPTER 15

# ON-BASE PLUS SLUGGING (OPS)

've spent the past fourteen chapters yelling at the neighborhood kids to get off my lawn, and I'm not backing down. It's a really nice lawn, and I've worked hard to keep it looking good. But sometimes even an old school baseball guy like me has to give credit where credit is due. While I still strongly believe that batting average is a more accurate reflection of a hitter's value than on-base percentage is (see chapter eight) and that RBIs matter (see chapter fourteen), I will concede that On-Base Plus Slugging, or OPS, is a useful metric when evaluating the performance of hitters.

On-Base Plus Slugging combines two seemingly unrelated stats, on-base percentage (calculated as times on base divided by plate appearances) and slugging percentage (calculated as total bases divided by at bats), into a single number that is intended to reflect a hitter's total offensive production. Only eight players in the history of the game have posted a career OPS greater than 1.0000 and, with the exception of Barry Bonds—a true outlier for reasons I won't go into here—the Angels' Mike Trout is the only one who has had an at-bat since 1960. Trout's career OPS is exactly 1.0000, good for eighth place all time, but a slight dip next season will take him below the mark for his career. The next closest active player on the list is Joey Votto of the Reds, whose career OPS of .9407 ranks him twenty-seventh all time.

While OPS might seem like a new statistic to some, it's actually been around for more than thirty years. Perhaps that's one of the reasons why I like it, or at least tolerate it. OPS first came to notoriety through the work of baseball author and researcher John Thorn, now the official historian of Major League Baseball, and statistician Pete Palmer in their 1984 book *The Hidden Game of Baseball*. It was further popularized when journalist Peter Gammons, my colleague at MLBN, started peppering his writing and television commentary with the term in the 1990s. OPS first appeared on a Topps baseball card—the standard bearer for all things statistical—in 2004 and has appeared on the backs of every Topps card since. Unlike UZR and other newfangled stats that have gone by the wayside, OPS appears to be here to stay.

It may seem unwise to include unequal values in an equation, and some have criticized proponents of OPS for that reason (stats wonks have posited that on-base percentage is actually 1.8 times more important than slugging percentage in terms of its effect on run scoring). It stands to reason that if the major league leaders in slugging are posting numbers between .600 and .700 for the most part but the league leaders in on-base percentage post numbers between 4.000 and 4.5000, then the OPS leaderboard will favor sluggers. It does, and that's kind of the point. Unlike batting average, which makes no distinction between a single and a home run, OPS proves that not all hits are created equal. And in 2019, when balls flew out of ballparks at a record rate (the 6,776 home runs hit in 2019 were 671 more than were hit in any previous season), five of the six players who finished among the top ten in on-base percentage, slugging, and OPS hit at least forty-one home runs. The fifth, Anthony Rendon of the Nationals, led the National League in both doubles and RBIs.

## PLAYERS WHO FINISHED AMONG THE TOP 10 LEADERS IN OBP, SLG, AND OPS IN 2019 BY HOME RUNS

|  | Home Runs |
|---|---|
| Cody Bellinger | 47 |
| Mike Trout | 45 |
| Christian Yelich | 44 |
| Alex Bregman | 41 |
| Nelson Cruz | 41 |
| Anthony Rendon | 34 |

Sabermetricians like OPS because it factors in the type of hits a batter produces. If a base hit is more valuable than a walk, which I believe it is, then so is an extra base hit more valuable than a single. Take, for example, a guy like Ichiro Suzuki. When the great Japanese import set a major league record with 262 hits for the Seattle Mariners in 2004, only thirty-seven of them went for extra bases. And even though he batted an astonishing .372 that season, he only drove in sixty runs, which is less than Rendon had at the all-star break this past season. Ichiro's OPS in that record-breaking season was .869, which was good enough to lead a ninety-nine-loss Mariners team but otherwise unremarkable. This is because in addition to his 225 singles he walked just forty-nine times, which for a leadoff hitter is an unusually low number. That low walk total contributed to Ichiro posting an on base percentage of only .4145 that year which, considering his hit total, is astonishingly low. When you combine that with his lack of extra base hits, the .869 OPS Ichiro put up that year is reflective of a player whose actual production was relatively minimal.

For comparison, let's again take a look at Trout. Before he got hurt early in the season's final month, he had an OPS of 1.083 in 2019. Compared to Ichiro his hit total (137) and batting average (.291) look pedestrian, yet he posted an American League-leading OPS because he had seventy-four extra base hits (exactly double the amount Ichiro had in 2004) in addition to 110 walks. Trout had also driven in 104 runs. Now obviously Ichiro and Trout are different kinds of players with different offensive skill sets, but the point I'm trying to make here is that while it's important, you can't look at batting average in a vacuum. Yes, Ichiro had a season for the ages in 2014, and I will always have a spot on my team for a guy who hits .372, but I'd rather have a hitter like Trout in my lineup every night of the week as well as in the doubleheader on Sunday, if they still played doubleheaders.

The goal of today's power hitters is to slug .600 or better while posting an on-base percentage of .400 or better. But even in baseball's current home run happy environment, this is easier said than done. Christian Yelich led the majors in OPS in 2019, posting a 1.1001 (.429 OBP, .671 SLG), and it was the highest average in the majors over the past three seasons. This is further proof that by combining two important stats, OPS provides a more accurate picture of who the game's elite offensive producers are. It's not a perfect stat by any means, and I'd never suggest that it replace good old batting average, home runs, and runs batted in as the standard barometers of a slugger's performance, but used in conjunction with those old school metrics, it definitely has a place. I'll give it that much.

Some in the analytics community believe that OPS+ or weighted on-base average (wOBA) are more accurate stats than plain old

Los Angeles Angels outfielder Mike Trout's 1.0000 career OPS ranks him eighth all time.

OPS because they account for outside factors, like park effects, that affect OPS scores, but I'm not going to go there. Stats that have plusses and minuses, weighting, and all kinds of funky formulas in them are, for an old school guy like me, a bridge too far.

Now get off my lawn.

# CHAPTER 16

# THE DESIGNATED HITTER

L et's go! It's time for Major League Baseball to have the National and American leagues play under the same rules and have the National League adopt the designated hitter. Playing by the same set of rules is reason enough for the DH to be in both leagues, but there are other reasons as well. Before we get to those, we need to go back in time a bit for a quick history lesson on why the two leagues are playing under different rules. Run scoring in Major League Baseball was down in the late 1960s, so MLB officials decided to lower the mound before the 1969 season. This gave pitchers less of an advantage over hitter and offenses enjoyed a brief uptick as a result, but as the 1972 season concluded they were trending back to 1968 norms.

• • •

| | Runs/GM | AVG | HR/GM |
|---|---|---|---|
| **MAJOR LEAGUE BASEBALL LEAGUE STATISTICS FROM 1968–1972** | | | |
| 1968 | 3.42 | .237 | 0.61 |
| **1969** | **4.07** | **.248** | **0.88** |
| 1970 | 4.34 | .254 | 0.88 |
| 1971 | 3.89 | .249 | 0.74 |
| 1972 | 3.69 | .244 | 0.68 |

*1969: Mound Was Lowered in Major League Baseball*

The designated hitter was tried in spring training for a few years and was called the "designated pinch hitter" in 1969 when four new expansion teams were added to the sport. When the idea was nixed after the 1972 season, both leagues put it up to a vote. On Jan. 11, 1973, the American League voted 8–4 in favor of adopting the designated hitter. At the time the American League was lagging behind the National League in attendance, and league officials thought the DH would give the sport a boost. The National League refused, however, considering the idea to be a gimmick.

In August of 1980, after seeing the AL's attendance and scoring increase, the National League held another vote. A simple majority was all that was needed to put the rule into place. The Pirates and Phillies vowed to vote as a bloc. Then Phillies owner Ruly Carpenter told his vice president, Bill Giles, to vote for the DH, because it would allow leftfielder Greg Luzinski to move to DH and provide young up-and-comer Keith Moreland with at-bats. But when the vote started, it was explained that the rule wouldn't go into place until 1982. Carpenter went fishing and Giles could not get ahold of him, so the Phillies abstained, as did the Pirates. The final vote tally was five against, four in favor, and three abstentions. If Giles would have just followed orders and not second-guessed, the National League would be playing with a DH today.

That's right. From 1982 until now, the DH would have been in place in both leagues. Major League Baseball is the only sport in which any subgroup of an entire league plays by a different rule. The National League requires pitchers to hit when two of its teams are playing against each other and when one is the host of an interleague game. In the latter case the American League team is forced to have its pitchers hit as well, even though they play with a DH. The fifteen teams that make up the National League are basically the only teams in *the entire* baseball world that play under these rules.

Triple-A baseball, one step away from the big leagues, is made up of two leagues: International and Pacific Coast. The International League is made up of three subgroups and the Pacific Coast League is made up of four subgroups. None of the seven subgroups in these two leagues are made up of entirely National League organizations, and whenever two AL affiliates face off, or an AL affiliate plays a NL affiliate, they use the DH. When two NL affiliates square off, however, the teams are given the option of using a DH or having their pitchers hit. Beyond those leagues, the rest of Minor League Baseball uses the DH full time. Professional leagues scattered throughout the world, such as in Japan, Korea, Mexico, and Australia all use the DH. At the amateur levels, all college and high school leagues use the DH. Pre-high school baseball made up of club, travel, and rec teams also use the DH. Knowing what the amateur baseball landscape looks like and coupling that with how the minor league rules operate up to and including AA baseball, a pitcher can find himself getting his first professional at-bat at the big league level. In some cases, this first professional at-bat might be his first at-bat since the age of fourteen. I can't see how this is good for baseball in any circumstance.

Pitchers have had a collective batting average hovering around .125 over the last few years. By comparison, designated hitters hit .247 in 2019 with 474 home runs.

| BATTING AVERAGE BY PITCHERS VS. DESIGNATED HITTERS—2014–2018 | | |
|---|---|---|
| | Pitchers | MLB DH |
| 2014 | .122 | .247 |
| 2015 | .132 | .259 |
| 2016 | .132 | .254 |
| 2017 | .124 | .244 |
| 2018 | .115 | .248 |

Consider the fact that the chief complaint of the union is that players in their thirties are not getting offers for jobs. Consider the fact that fifteen teams don't even entertain signing older players because of their likely fielding deficiencies. Recently guys like Nelson Cruz and Mark Reynolds were signed to either one-year or minor league deals because a lot of the American League teams already had their designated hitter spot filled. If baseball is looking to create more jobs and boost offense, it needs to play under one set of rules and the National League should adopt the DH.

The arguments from the staunch National League supporters I hear revolve around the sentiment "There's more strategy and it's just a better game" with the pitcher hitting. The strategy part of this seems to point toward several different things: the manager's decisions regarding removing pitchers, the bunt, the double switch, and the pitcher's spot in the lineup. Let's break those things down:

# DEBUNKING THE IDEA THAT THERE IS "MORE STRATEGY IN NATIONAL LEAGUE GAMES"

## Manager's Decisions Regarding Removing the Pitcher

In most cases the scoreboard calls for the manager to make a pitching change. If a team is down two runs in the sixth inning or later and has a man on base with the pitcher due up, National League managers will invariably hit for the pitcher regardless of how well he is pitching. But American League managers managing in a DH rule game will base their pitching change decisions on whether he thinks his pitcher still has something left in the tank and remains the best choice to face the opponent's next hitters. This type of a decision requires much more strategy and feel for the game than pitching change decisions in the National League do, since in many cases the NL manager's decision is dictated by outside factors.

## The Bunt

The ability to bunt has basically gone by the wayside in the game today. It's a lost art, and asking a pitcher to get a bunt down in a critical situation has become more and more unfair to the pitcher. He simply hasn't had the reps in his past and certainly doesn't get the reps now that he needs to be efficient at bunting. Practicing off of a machine on the back fields of a spring training facility doesn't really relate to facing a guy throwing ninety-five-mile-per-hour heat with a slider.

## The Double Switch

Employing a double switch to favorably reset a team's batting order during a pitching change means that a manager is choosing to take a starting player out of his lineup. This starting player might be one of the better players on the field and, depending on when he is removed from the game, he might miss out on a couple of at-bats before it's decided. How can removing a good player from the game be good for the game? This may fall under "strategy," but it looks like a not so productive tool to me. Consider the 2018 National League Wild Card Game: Rockies manager Bud Black double switched Charlie Blackmon out of the game so he could get length out of his reliever. In order to get two innings out of a pitcher, Buddy removed from the lineup one of his best hitters (and at the time his hottest bat).

## The Pitcher's Spot in Lineup

Here's a situation we see just about every night in a National League game. There's a runner on second base with two out. With the opposing pitcher on deck, the hitter at the plate is walked. The pitcher then strikes out, ending the inning. Enough said.

In the National League we have also become accustomed to seeing star pitchers who are gate attractions get removed from a game for a pinch hitter because he fell behind early. This pitcher got back on track and is pitching really well, but because the scoreboard and the "book" dictate it, he gets the hook. If I were the owner of a big league team and made a large investment in a pitcher, I would want him pitching as much as possible. I don't need to see him hit one time, and I certainly do not want to watch the guy running the bases and sliding. Starting pitchers are throwing fewer innings than ever before. In 2008 eight different pitchers threw at least 220 innings, but in 2018 there was only one, Max

The Nationals' Max Scherzer was the only pitcher in the major leagues to throw at least 220 innings in 2018. In 2019, Justin Verlander was the only one.

Scherzer. Let's take away one of the things that are shortening the starters' outings by instituting the DH in both leagues.

The main reason for having the DH adopted by the National League is to simply play by the same set of rules. In addition to this, it makes even more sense knowing that the entire world at all amateur and professional levels plays with the DH. Lastly, if the game needs more offense, the DH will be better at putting up offensive numbers than the pitcher will.

# CHAPTER 17

# THE GAME BEING PLAYED

The talent of the players competing in the game today has never been better. The individual skills and abilities of these players need to be celebrated. While I still believe the game hasn't changed all that much, we are truly seeing things in this game that we have never seen before. Younger and younger players are now making their big league debuts regularly. We are seeing young position players put up offensive numbers that compare to the production of some of the game's greatest players. Most pitchers are throwing mid- to upper-nineties and a select few are even reaching triple digits. Baseball has never seen this much talent out of the position player pool or velocity from the guys on the bump. The individual player has raised the bar as far as eye-popping, "What did I just see?" moments go. But is the actual game being played by these super-talented guys better than it was twenty-five years ago? I'm not so sure. While the players truly are better than ever, I do have concerns about some of the finer points of the game.

All thirty major league teams are affected by these concerns in one way or another, possibly multiple times. Players make up the team, but each team also has a manager, coaches, and a front office full of executives. Every major league organization has at least five minor league affiliates that develop talent to feed into their big league team. So if there are any flaws with how the game is played or how things are executed on the baseball field, it might not be as simple as to point at a single player and say, "How could he do that?" Examined on an island the player might look like a guilty party, but he encountered many influencers on the way to that island.

Let's look at a situation in which there's a base runner on first base and two outs. He tries to go first to third on a base hit but gets thrown out making the third out at third base. In yesteryear, that violated one of the game's golden rules: "Never make the first or last out of an inning at third base." I believe this should still be a golden rule and if it's a rule teams still adhere to, I must be missing something, because I see this kind of out being made every night. The player making this out at third base is responsible for his own action, but his influencers can be traced back to every one of his minor league managers and coaches as well as to his manager and coaches on the big league team. His decision to try for third should also be directly tied to the situation at hand. If a runner is on first with two outs, the first base coach should verbally say to him, "Don't make the last out at third!" This verbal reminder should have happened every time this same situation presented itself in the minor leagues, and it should happen every time it happens in the big leagues now. If organizations still value this golden rule, a ten-year major league vet who spent four years in the minor leagues should have heard "Don't make the last out at third!" at least five hundred times.

There are a few scenarios in which I'm okay with an inning ending with an out at third base (or possibly in between second and third base). These specific situations should be verbally communicated to the base runner at the time they arise. One of them could be if there are runners on first and second with two outs, down a run, in the seventh inning, and there's a base hit. If the runner on first base sees the runner on second base being sent home by the third base coach and he feels that there is a good chance that runner will be out at home plate, he can head toward third base to force a cut off and have the defense make a play on him instead of at home. If this happens, he cannot blindly run into third base and get tagged out before the run scores. This is where stopping and getting into a rundown comes into play. It's a situation that calls for you to trade an out for a run, since that run ties the game.

If some in the new school have determined that this golden rule is no longer relevant to today's game, this can be disputed as well. Leading off an inning with a double and making the first out at third base trying to stretch it into a triple is just not worth the risk. I really can't think of a situation in which I would reverse my position on making the first out at third base. The scoreboard should play a major role in the player's thoughts and decisions, of course, not just on the offensive side of the ball but when playing defense as well.

Another form of making ill-advised outs is when a base runner decides to go into "I'm gonna keep running until I get tagged out" mode. This usually happens when he has an RBI on the line. With a runner on second base, the batter gets a base hit to right field. On this possible scoring play, the throw from right field is heading to home plate, and the batter just keeps running and mindlessly runs into a pointless out. This type of an out has turned into somewhat of an epidemic throughout baseball, and it seems to be very contagious. The more runners on base and the more possible RBIs there are to be had, the better. You can almost bet the farm that a player who hits a bases-loaded double and picks up three runs batted in will either be safe at third base on a throw to home plate or out at third base as a result of the defense executing simple alignments and throws. If all thirty teams could execute some simple defensive routines better than they do now, base runners would make even more outs than they do right now.

I am in awe of all the talent in the big leagues today and how easy these players can make something look, because I know firsthand how hard the game is to play. The overall crispness of play is a little bit of a concern to me, though. I believe as with most everything else that there are a number of factors that influence why we don't—or can't—put our best foot forward or be the best version of ourselves or team that we can be. For the individual player, talent can only get you so far toward being the best you can be. But if that talented player gets quality mental and physical instruction along the way, and puts in the time and effort to improve, his talent will shine even more. For the team, putting players in the best possible positions to succeed while continuing to develop talent will enhance each player's ultimate value to the team. If all players perform better, the team as a whole will be better.

Games played in the minor leagues are extremely important toward the development of the complete player. It's about experiencing as many baseball situations as possible. Having knowledgeable baseball people in place who have the ability to teach is vital in pointing out what to do in these key situations. If the player makes a mistake of any kind and it's not pointed out, the player doesn't know it was a mistake. With so many new thoughts and practices being integrated into the game, we cannot lose sight of the baseball's fundamentals and how the game should be played.

| MINOR LEAGUE GAMES PLAYED | | |
| --- | --- | --- |
| | Games | At-Bats |
| Eddie Murray | 449 | 1,558 |
| Cal Ripken Jr. | 443 | 1,652 |
| Chipper Jones | 456 | 1,679 |
| Derek Jeter | 447 | 1,751 |
| Bryce Harper | 130 | 591 |
| Manny Machado | 219 | 820 |
| Juan Soto | 122 | 453 |
| Ronald Acuna Jr. | 259 | 1,002 |

The minor league games played and at bats for the four Hall of Famers (Murray, Ripken, Jones, and Jeter) in the above table certainly helped them on their respective journeys to Cooperstown. Mistakes were made in a developmental environment, and the players learned valuable lessons from those mistakes. Experiencing almost every game situation in a place where it is understandable if wrong decisions are made is what the minor leagues are for. The four youngsters breezed through the minor league system because they were really advanced and probably more talented and skilled than the Hall of Famers were at that same age.

These young guys are possibly experiencing game situations for the very first time under the spotlight of the big leagues. In some ways this is a little unfair, as these guys have so much responsibility and pressure thrust upon them at such young ages. What's incredible, and most impressive, is how often they rise to the challenge.

I battled some injuries early in my minor league career, and I never had the talent that guys like Acuna and Soto possess, but I

Juan Soto was just nineteen years old when he made his
major league debut for the Washington Nationals in 2018.

couldn't even fathom what it would have been like to play in the
major leagues at nineteen. The things I learned both on and off
the field in terms of playing the game and growing as a person
prepared me to succeed to the best of my ability when I finally did
get my call to the show, and I am grateful for that experience.

# CHAPTER 18

# THE CONTROL GROUP

It seems to me that with all the experimentation going on in today's game, there needs to be a control group. If research scientists won't call something an experiment unless there's a control group, baseball should require the same. To draw any real conclusions from an experiment, there must be truthful information and facts that influence the conclusion. The best way to determine if outside elements have any effect on an experiment is to have something in the experiment that cannot be influenced. Having an organization's analytics department say "This is what we do" is one thing, but do we know if that's really what's being done by the players on the field? There are teams, like the Astros and Rays, that have a reputation for being on the cutting edge of analyzing everything, and the information that gets passed down to their dugouts is pretty darn close to can't miss. It's mind-blowing stuff. But how do we know that the players are using all this info? We don't, but because there is this overwhelmingly analytical, propaganda-based message being delivered through some of the media, it's believed that players in these organizations are succeeding largely because the numbers given to them allowed for it.

It would be extremely difficult to have a perfect control group in major league baseball, as none of the thirty big league teams are created equal to begin with. Payroll and market size are the biggest influencers on how teams can be very different. We're always going to have variances, but if baseball were ever to enforce a salary cap and floor, that would help in leveling out the playing field. That's probably not going to happen any time soon, though, so how can we turn one of the thirty major league teams into the best possible control group for a "game-changing" experiment?

Well, first we'd need one of the ownership groups to be willing to participate in the experiment, which in my opinion would be one of coolest in the history of American sports. This is where I could offer up my services. If one of these franchise owners would be willing to give me the keys to the castle, I would cut my brother Cal Jr. a set of those keys and it would be on!

Why would a major league owner or ownership group entertain this idea? It's simple: It would work. Neither my brother nor I have front office experience, but between the two of us, we have people we really like in our circle who do have front office experience and the track records that go with it. With a front office in place, there's no doubt in my mind that we could evaluate what we have in the entire organization and make the necessary baseball operations moves in a timely and efficient manner. There are quality baseball people who would line up for the opportunity to get back into an old school baseball organization. Quite a few guys have been pushed away from this game for one reason or another, and some of these guys would make a comeback for sure with our group.

I could guarantee that our organization, from top down, would be the old school control group that this experiment would need.

Some teams with analytics-minded leadership have had success, but how can we be sure that this success can be attributable to their new school approach? If every team is moving in the same direction, there's nothing to compare this new approach to. When all teams are zigging, it's time for a team to zag, especially if the zag means returning to an old school approach toward playing the game. As I wrote in this book's introduction, an old school approach isn't just throwing bats and balls onto the field and saying "Go get 'em." Quite to the contrary, an old school approach means gathering and analyzing all of the information at your disposal while using baseball common sense to determine whether the information can be applied. I believe there are some teams that do this some of the time, but the perception that some teams' analytics departments rule the roost is reality as well. My new hypothetical squad would remove all doubt regarding which school was in charge and would therefore be the best possible team to have as the experiment's control group.

If this idea intrigues any one of the thirty major league team owners, who want to win and possibly put their names in the history books, have your people call my people and we can set up a face-to-face meeting over steaks and beers. We could technically do this, in this day and age, with electronic communication, but I don't believe there is a better way to get things done than a good, old-fashioned sit-down with some good food and a libation or two or three. Terms of our agreement could even be agreed upon and written down on a cocktail napkin during our first sit-down.

I'm already on the record saying that I believe World Series teams of the past and the present were built in the same way, and it is with this belief in mind that one of my first courses of action as president of baseball operations would take place. Targeting the draft and development aspect of my new organization will be imperative. This will help to create a core of young players that I will be able to build upon to create a championship club. Our draft would heavily involve my scouting department, which will be composed of experienced baseball guys who have been hitting the bushes for years and know what they're looking for.

My developmental team of managers and coaches will probably be smaller in number than what current major league organizations are supporting right now. Reducing the number of coaches in my minor leagues will also reduce the number of voices—and noise in general—that my minor league players will hear. I'm not looking at reducing payroll with these cuts. In fact, I will pay the coaches I do hire more as I'm going to give each of them more responsibility. These managers and coaches stationed at the various minor league cities will be given their marching orders, which will include a command to "teach these boys how to play." That phrase might seem vague to some, but to the guys I would hire and trust to carry out my mission, it will be very clear.

The manager, pitching coach, and hitting coach will be staples at all classifications, from rookie league to AAA. Every classification will have the same level of importance placed upon it. With this approach I'm sure I can fill out my minor league staff with high quality and character individuals. Organizational roving instructors and special assistants will play a role as they are needed, but my three "everyday boots-on-the-ground workers" in every minor league town will carry most of the weight with the development of these players.

The approach and style of our organization will resemble what my dad and others like him were charged with doing back in the day, and like them we will teach our young ballplayers the right way to play. We will teach them to be professionals. The talent level of today's young amateur players is better than that of their predecessors. I get this and I acknowledge this. But I don't think they necessarily play the game better. The young players playing under my developmental staff will understand that regardless of their talent, how they go about their business and how they play the game matters. The daily reinforcement of information, common sense, and experience will guide these players toward their ultimate goal of becoming big league players. The information we'll use will not be the atom-splitting type, though. Instead it will revolve around analyzing what has transpired in past games and how best to apply that knowledge moving forward. Learning through playing the game and figuring out things on their own will serve our players better than studying spreadsheets. The manager at each level will be the headman for sure, and whenever a visit is made by a rover or a special assistant, a total collaboration will be in play. These visits might have even come about as a result of a special need by the manager, meaning support for his mission is needed. Parallel tracks are certainly going to be running at the same time as we set this control experiment in motion, but you'll have to read my next book (or hire me) for those. World Series teams are built through the draft and then developed into the core of a winning team, and I believe I could do that with a little help from my friends.

I'll even drive the bus.

# CHAPTER 19

# POSITIONAL VERSATILITY, BENCH PLAYERS, AND PLATOONING

**P**ositional versatility is a newfangled term used to describe ball-players who have the ability to play multiple positions. Utility men, as we used to call them, are not new to baseball, though. There are a select few players in the big leagues who own multiple gloves, play more than one position, and play every day. If any of these guys have a chance at being great at one position, I'd like to see them get a chance to do so. If I have a great defensive first base-man and he happens to also be really good at right field, I'd choose great over really good. If a replacement first baseman is good and forces my great first baseman to right field, I just traded great for good and that just doesn't make any sense at all to me. I don't want to rotate bald tires on my truck. Along those lines, if you've got one good tire and you keep rotating that one good tire around your truck that's not good either. I've stated my case earlier in this book that a first baseman is much more valuable defensively than any outfielder, so if you give me a great first baseman, he will own only one glove and will be manning that position every day.

The Cubs' Kris Bryant may be the player most responsible for this now popular description of a player's value and ability to use multiple gloves. Primarily a third baseman, Bryant won the National League Rookie of the Year award in 2015 and the National League MVP award the following year, when he led the Cubs to their first World Series title in 108 years. But while Bryant started 136 games at third base as a rookie, he saw time at first base, all three outfield positions, and even shortstop during his MVP sophomore campaign. This have-glove-will-travel utility necessitated a term, and thus positional versatility was born. Let's take a look back at games started by Bryant in his first two major league seasons.

## KRIS BRYANT GAMES STARTED BY POSITION—2015–2016

|  | 2015 | 2016 |
| --- | --- | --- |
| Third Base | 136 | 100 |
| Left Field | 4 | 36 |
| Center Field | 1 | 0 |
| Right Field | 5 | 12 |
| First Base | 1 | 6 |
| Designated Hitter | 1 | 0 |

Obviously, there must have been a *need* to have the 2015 National League Rookie of the Year become more versatile defensively. Trust me, Bryant didn't win the MVP award the next season because he started fifty-four games at a position other than third base. If you move a back-to-back award winner away from his primary position, it must be to make room for a future Hall of Famer, right? While Bryant led all National League third

The Cubs' Kris Bryant is, in some ways, the poster boy for
positional versatility, but I believe he should be entrenched at third base.

basemen in errors in 2017, I cannot be convinced that moving
Kris Bryant off third base to create playing time for different players was ever a good idea. I also can't imagine that the Cubs going
to the postseason and winning it all was a result of Bryant playing
different positions throughout the year.

In fact, when the 2016 Cubs reached the playoffs, Bryant
started all seventeen games at third base with the Cubs on their
way to becoming World Champions. This tells me that the Cubs
were at their best when Bryant played third base.

A bench player or extra man is a little different; he doesn't play 150–160 games a year. Instead, he may find himself with sixty-eighty games played by year's end. This guy, in playing two to three times a week, might find himself in left field, right field, and at third base in his three games for the week. I get the value of his versatility and the thought process behind carrying a player like this on one's roster. But I also believe that there's no need to overdose on this new toy term, *positional versatility*. Excessive defensive juggling and individual pinballing can't be the most effective way get your best defensive team on the field. Having guys play a defensive position that best suits them is the best way to field your best defensive team. The overall game will be better for this as well.

Comfort, consistency, and familiarity are important to baseball players. Conversely, uncertainty and surprises can negatively impact a player's performance. I can guarantee you that an everyday shortstop prefers his double-play partner and his third baseman to be consistent as well. Continuity, over the course of a long season, matters.

As I mentioned above, bench or back-up infielders were simply listed as utility players back in the day. In the outfield, they were simply called fourth or fifth outfielders. These guys were typically good defenders and were used to give an everyday player a day off or to fill in when a starter got dinged up or hit the disabled list. It wasn't that common back then for a back-up infielder to play an outfield position, and I really can't remember a fourth outfielder ever coming in to play an infield position unless there was an emergency. In some cases, the twenty-fourth or twenty-fifth player on the roster really didn't play that much, especially in the American League, if he was on a club built with a stable of everyday guys.

In 1996, when I played for the Orioles, we were pretty set at every position: Rafael Palmeiro at first base, Roberto Alomar at second base, Jr. at short, and B.J. Surhoff at third base. When Surhoff went down in late May with a sprained left ankle, I played the next thirteen games at third. I hit pretty well, batting .300 with two homers, did not commit an error in thirty-six chances, and our team went 8–5 during that span. I'm not saying the record had anything to do with me, but by playing every day I did not take anything away from the team. When B.J. came back from the DL, I knew my role on the team was to serve as a utility infielder, and I didn't have any claim to a starting spot on the infield. I knew Raffy was at first, Robby was at second, Jr. was at short, and B.J. was the starting third baseman. As they should have been.

The point of the "extra man" back then was for him to remain largely unnoticed. Their positive contributions were appreciated, but it was more about not standing out in a negative way. The exception to this is the defensive replacement, who might enter a game in late innings to help defend a lead.

Platooning is an old school term that describes a situation in which a team might have two players at the same position who are about equal in terms of their defensive ability but hit from opposite sides of the plate. If the splits (right-handed hitter versus left-handed pitcher and left-handed hitter versus right-handed pitcher) were heavily favorable, the platoon was employed. For the most part, platoon players were limited to that one position as it was each player's primary and best position.

## 1983 BALTIMORE ORIOLES—LEFT FIELD

|  | G | AVG | OPS | HR |
|---|---|---|---|---|
| John Lowenstein | 98 | .279 | .841 | 13 |
| Gary Roenicke | 45 | .302 | .979 | 15 |

## 1986 NEW YORK METS—CENTER FIELD

|  | G | AVG | OPS | XBH |
|---|---|---|---|---|
| Lenny Dykstra | 98 | .298 | .831 | 39 |
| Mookie Wilson | 57 | .319 | .852 | 22 |

## 1993 PHILADELPHIA PHILLIES—LEFT FIELD

|  | G | AVG | OPS | HR |
|---|---|---|---|---|
| Pete Incaviglia | 80 | .278 | .884 | 22 |
| Milt Thompson | 78 | .265 | .700 | 4 |

## 1993 PHILADELPHIA PHILLIES—RIGHT FIELD

|  | G | AVG | OPS | HR |
|---|---|---|---|---|
| Jim Eisenrich | 77 | .316 | .807 | 7 |
| Wes Chamberlain | 73 | .290 | .842 | 12 |

Traditional platoons make much more sense to me than the Swiss Army knives being deployed in today's game defensive alignments. An actual Swiss Army knife will allow you to do a multitude of things. You can cut a small limb, tighten a screw, open a can, or even scale a fish. With that said I still want a lumberjack playing third, a screw gun at short, an electric can opener at second, and a leather-faced fishmonger playing first. The right tool for the job is important in getting the job done right. The Swiss Army knife will do in a pinch and, with some effort, can get the job done. But if the knife gets over used and the job is too big for the multitool, it will break down.

# CHAPTER 20

# UNWRITTEN RULES

The game of baseball dates back to the mid-nineteenth century, and over the years there have been many situations that have caused some hard feelings between the teams playing on any given day. These moments within the game have created a somewhat universal and accepted code of conduct that exists beyond the margins of the game's official rulebook. The usual punishment or retribution for breaking some of these rules was and remains a batter wearing one from the pitcher. Is this a somewhat barbaric thing to do? Maybe, but in my opinion, having this option available has enabled the game to maintain a level of respect and normalcy. The unwritten rules of baseball have never been codified—hence the word "unwritten"—or publicized much, but almost everyone playing the game understands when a violation has occurred. The reason I said "almost everyone" is because a 100 percent complete understanding of anything is extremely rare, if not impossible. When a player or a team acts outside of the unwritten yet accepted rules for how the game should be played, an opposing player or team will invariably send a message by taking matters into their own hands. This retaliation is rarely a surprise to anyone involved, including the umpires, and they sometimes result in ejections. But they serve to reinforce the accepted code of what you can do and what you can't do in the game.

This system has been in place and used by players since the game began. Have there been incidents over the years that have gotten out of hand and been downright dangerous? You bet. Competitive sports being played at the highest level will always have moments of danger and the risk of injury. Even the most competitive athletes can accept that losing is part of the game, but what they can't accept is being disrespected. And when major leaguers feel as if an opponent is trying to show them up or attack them personally, it will open the door for some extracurricular activity.

The phrase "Let the players police themselves" gets mocked and ridiculed the most by people who never played the game. But if the players themselves—guys who have everything invested in the sport—don't have a problem with policing the game, why should anyone outside of that group have a say regarding how it's done? Have members of this outside group ever competed at something in the way the professional athletes they're watching do?

While most ballplayers who come out on the short end of the stick are able to handle defeat well as an individual or on a team, there will be and always have been players who will push the envelope regarding what is considered offensive by the majority of their fellow players.

In other sports, fouls or penalties are often levied against the second offender, the retaliator, while the initial offender sometimes gets away with starting something. In football, it could be after the play, when one guys decides to give a subtle head butt to another guy's face mask. When the recipient of the head butt retaliates with a two-handed shove to the chest, he gets flagged for a fifteen-yard unsportsmanlike conduct penalty. In hockey a quick, well-placed slash might find a delicate spot on an opposing player's wrist, but if the slashed player's reaction is a more forceful and easily detectable retaliation slash, he's the one who gets called for a two-minute minor. In basketball, an offensive big man's elbow might connect with a defender's ribs while they are battling for position on the low block, but if the defender responds with a forceful forearm to the elbower's lower back, he's the one who'll get whistled for the personal foul. These examples are not quite the same as when someone pimps a home run and then takes a fastball to his ribs his next time up. But all of the above examples are similar in terms of cause-and-effect. If the first action did not take place, the second action would not have taken place either.

There are a few guys in the current game who feel that putting a little extra flair on top of an on-field achievement is necessary or appropriate. It doesn't appear to occur to these select few that doing one's job well is good enough. They feel a need to rub that achievement in their opponents' faces, which naturally and justifiably rubs some guys the wrong way. The two main outcomes that seem to elicit these demonstrations of flair most often are the punch out and the home run. Some offenders try to excuse their behavior by saying that they're just having fun out there, and I can understand that to a degree. Baseball is supposed to be fun, but there is and always will be a fine line between having fun and going overboard with a "look at me" display of poor sportsmanship. Flair has been creeping into the game over the last few years and I believe—correctly so—that it has been met with some resistance, specifically by old school types. This resistance has not been received well or even understood by some, and this, too, is to be expected. Unanimity in opinion is a tough thing to achieve in anything, much less in a sport marked by cultural and generational divides. That said, I still believe that the majority in the game know what's going on and understand why things are still done a certain way.

I don't want to see baseball turn into a game in which players celebrate over every little thing they do. I'm all for having fun when the situation warrants it, but the last thing baseball needs is to emulate the NFL, where a player whose team is down three scores in the fourth quarter will make a routine tackle and do some crazy "look at me" dance as if his team is up by three scores. That's definitely not good for the game. All the people who say "Look at football's popularity" can go cover football full time. Baseball will survive without them.

I will never question a release of pure emotion or a genuine reaction to doing something well so long as it's within the bounds of good sportsmanship. Dugout celebrations are becoming more and more over the top, but I'm starting to view these as the boys just having fun in their own space. In my opinion, these celebrations are not in your face, "look what I just did to you" type displays in the same way as a pitcher doing a disco spin move after a punchie or a hitter styling and profiling at the dish after going deep is. If these two acts of self-congratulation are allowed to continue happening, the pace of play won't improve and extracurricular incidents occurring in between actual game-play will increase. I say this because the individuals participating in the antics seem to be the ones who get just as offended as anyone else.

The fine line and the cause-and-effect phenomenon aren't exclusive to baseball; they exist in our everyday lives. For example, let's go for a drive. No matter what roadway we hit, there's a pretty good chance that we'll exceed the speed limit. Now let's hit the highway. You know that 65 MPH is the speed limit on this highway, but do you actually go 65 MPH? Do you instead hover around 70 MPH with the idea that going 5 MPH over the limit is no big deal, or are you the driver who sets his cruise control at 74 believing that going 9 MPH over the limit isn't worthy of a cop pulling you over? Is 79 MPH your threshold for violating the speed limit with the belief that 80 MPH is the magic pull-over number, or are you the type to roll the dice and take the chance that you can go 85 MPH without attracting flashing lights? If you never speed, I feel pretty confident in saying that you won't get a ticket. But if, conversely, you're really heavy footed, your chance of getting a ticket is fairly high. That's the risk you take when you make the decision to speed.

When pushing the envelope, we all should know there is a cut-off point or a point where you can push things too far. And when you reach that point there are consequences. If we don't understand this, problems will occur for sure in many situations. If you hit a homer, drop the bat, and trot around the bases at a respectful pace, I don't believe you should ever worry about getting drilled your next time up. But if you hit a homer, flip the bat, admire your shot, and then lollygag around the bases, there's a pretty good chance that you will end up wearing one in the ribs at some point. There's a fine line to toe when you're on the road, just like there is for hitters in the batter's box. Rolling the dice can be an iffy proposition.

# CHAPTER 21

# RUN DIFFERENTIAL

Run differential is nothing more than the difference between the number of runs your team scores and the number of runs it allows. It has been around for a long time and has been included with the standings for years. The other major sports use this stat in their standings as well. More recently it has been used in baseball as a predictor of a team's possible win-loss record and as a blanket assessment of a team's performance. Former NFL head coach Bill Parcells said it best: "You are what your record says you are." This certainly holds true in today's game no matter what your run differential is.

A first-place team in any division that is killing it record-wise is usually among the best in run differential. A first-place team is usually a first-place team because it has both good pitching and good hitting. This means it doesn't give up many runs and it can score a lot. This isn't rocket science, and the reverse is also true. The last place team in any division doesn't pitch or hit well, meaning they give up a lot of runs and don't score very many. Do we really need any other stats appearing in the agate type besides wins, losses, games back, and "last ten"? I don't think so. You are what you are! If we feel a need to have other numbers in the standings other than wins and losses, we should be able to explain why certain teams might have a good or bad record with a conflicting run differential.

Those who most often regurgitate run differential statistics rarely have this explanation. They simply say things like, "This team should be better because of their run differential" or "This team isn't that good; look at their run differential." Once again, this is implying that one plus one in baseball equals two. But not everything in baseball can be explained through an equation. Too many variables come into play when talking about baseball and any one individual team's success or failure. The first-place teams and the last-place teams do, most of the time, fall in line with run differential. The teams in the middle of the standings usually fall into place as well, with a few exceptions. These exceptions need to be examined under a baseball microscope, not an analytical one. There are reasons why certain teams find ways to win one-or-two run games more often than others do. Teams that lose those one-run games just might be good enough to lose. A team winning a three-game series with game scores of 3–2, 2–0, 1–7 will have a -3 run differential while going 2–1. This kind of series does happen, and if it happens multiple times, the numbers start to add up.

The small sample sizes combine to make up the long season. Having a few good bullpen pieces but not a complete bullpen, as many teams today do, could lead to such a series. The same could happen if you have two good starting pitchers but the rest of your rotation is questionable. The execution of simple but sometimes overlooked fundamentals by the offense or defense could come into play as well. This could be something as simple as an offensive player not making a productive out and at least advancing a runner ninety feet late in a game when the score is tied. Or it could be a defensive player making an ill-advised throw to the wrong base and allowing an opposing player to get an extra base. We have seen appearances by position players as pitchers earlier and earlier in the past few baseball seasons. Could this be a phone-it-in mentality by some teams throwing in the towel and saving its bullpen in lopsided games? Do teams sometimes lose a battle to try to win the war? Yes they do, especially contenders. Is there any difference in the standings between a one-run loss and a ten-run loss? No. We need to examine every team by how they are constructed.

A team that's close to a .500 can find itself with either a positive or negative run differential. Should we look at a team with a higher run differential that is third in a division more favorably than the second-place team in that same division that has a lower run differential? No. I believe that teams that "should be better" than their record shows based on a favorable run differential are not actually better than they have shown. I also believe that the teams that finish with a record better than what their run differential indicates might just be good teams that find a way to win the close games. Most playoff teams will end up posting impressive run differential numbers in the standings column, but isn't this just common sense? Sure it is. Most teams that go 91–71 over a 162-game season will also look good in the run differential column; however, do not discount a team that makes the playoffs with a run differential that doesn't jump off the board at you. They could be just as dangerous. Teams win and lose games for reasons that can and should be explained, but just throwing out run differential numbers doesn't get it done.

A team's goal should be to win every game they play. This can change quickly as games unfold, though. This isn't about throwing a game or tanking, it's just the reality of the sport. If the game doesn't go as desired or planned and you find yourself down by what seems to be an insurmountable deficit, it's time to start thinking about how best to set yourself up for the next day or two, so that one loss doesn't become two or three. And if your team's run differential takes a hit as a result, so be it.

# CHAPTER 22

# LINEUP CONSTRUCTION

In years past and throughout the game's history, teams constructed their lineups very similarly. Baseball teams have always paid attention to what everyone else was doing, and if something worked for one team it might work for another. For many years, the first five guys in most batting orders could generally be defined or identified as follows:

1. The leadoff guy had some speed, could steal a base, and generally was a pain in the backside for the opposing pitcher. Part of being a PITA was seeing pitches and being a distraction when on base.

2. The guy in the two spot was someone who could handle the bat a bit and be capable of bunting to move a man over. Using the hit-and-run was fairly common as well with this guy, especially with the leadoff guy having some speed on base in front of him.

3. The third hitter was the team's best overall hitter. He was expected to hit .300 and score and drive in a hundred runs a year.

4. The four hole was reserved for your cleanup guy; in most cases the biggest home run totals came out of this spot in the order, and the slugger filling this slot usually hit somewhere in the neighborhood of .280 on the year.

5. The fifth spot was similar to the bopper in front of him. Maybe not with quite as much power, but he was as stubborn as any guy in the lineup and possessed both the desire and ability to drive in runs.

Managers ran these five guys out there every day, invariably in their same spots in the order and the same positions in the field.

Let's take a look at the 1990–92 Pittsburgh Pirates' most regularly used lineups as they were winning the National League's eastern division under manager Jim Leyland.

## 1990 PITTSBURGH PIRATES—REGULAR STARTING LINEUP (USED MOST BY TEAM)

1. 3B Wally Backman: 104 games, 62 runs, 92 hits
2. SS Jay Bell: 39 Sac Bunts, 93 runs
3. CF Andy Van Slyke: 77 RBI, 67 runs
4. RF Bobby Bonilla: 120 RBI, 112 Runs
5. LF Barry Bonds: 114 RBI, 104 Runs
6. 1B Sid Bream
7. C Mike LaValliere
8. 2B José Lind
9. Pitcher's spot

## 1991 PITTSBURGH PIRATES—REGULAR STARTING LINEUP (USED MOST BY TEAM)

1. 1B Orlando Merced: Scored 83 runs
2. SS Jay Bell: 30 Sac bunts, 96runs
3. CF Andy Van Slyke: 83 RBI, 87 Runs
4. 3B Bobby Bonilla: 100 RBI, 102 Runs
5. LF Barry Bonds: 117 RBI, 95 Runs
6. RF Gary Varsho
7. C Mike LaValliere
8. 2B José Lind
9. Pitcher's spot

## 1992 PITTSBURGH PIRATES—REGULAR STARTING LINEUP (USED MOST BY TEAM)

1. RF Alex Cole: 64 Games, 33 Runs, 57 Hits
2. SS Jay Bell: 19 Sac Bunts, 87 Runs
3. CF Andy Van Slyke: 89 RBI, 103 Runs
4. LF Barry Bonds: 103 RBI, 109 Runs
5. 1B Orlando Merced: 60 RBI
6. 3B Jeff King
7. C Mike LaValliere
8. 2B José Lind
9. Pitcher's spot

In these three years, the Pirates pretty much stayed true to the old school definition of lineup configuration. It wasn't perfect, but it was consistent. More than that, it succeeded, resulting in 289 regular season wins. Each player in the lineup knew their role and what was expected of them. Comfort and chemistry grew out of the consistency, and the lineup produced as a team and for the team instead of producing for any one of the individuals, including Barry Bonds. Jay Bell gave himself up when asked to do so by laying down eighty-eight sacrifice bunts over these three years. That would make the new school of today cringe, but back then it made Jim Leyland and every other member of those Pirates teams applaud. In the 1991 season, Bell had thirty sac bunts with fifteen of those coming in the first inning! The Buccos scored in nine of those first innings. That was how this team was built and their three straight National League East titles tells me that they were built really well. When the whole is greater than the sum of its parts, that's the mark of a true team.

In those days, the intimidating and feared sluggers who hit in the four spot in the batting order were as well known as the opening day starting pitchers on most teams, if not better known. Eddie Murray, Fred McGriff, Juan González, Will Clark, Darryl Strawberry, Albert Belle, Dave Winfield, and Jim Thome were everyday four-hole hitters capable of doing damage in every at bat, and every baseball fan knew it. Earl Weaver liked pitching, defense, and the three-run homer, and Eddie Murray was a part of that formula in Baltimore for years.

Eddie hit 173 two-run home runs, sixty-five three-run home runs, and nineteen grand slams in his career. That's 257 out of his 504 career home runs. So a little more than 50 percent of his home runs were multiple-run homers. The nineteen slams are the fourth most in history, behind only Alex Rodriguez, Lou Gehrig, and Manny Ramírez. And I'll take a three-run home run over two solo home runs any day of the week.

Before Barry Bonds started putting up cartoon numbers as a member of the San Francisco Giants, the seven-time National League MVP was at the heart of a Pittsburgh Pirates lineup that won three consecutive division titles.

Hall of Famer Eddie Murray's nineteen career grand slams
are the fourth most in major league baseball history.

The sixth and seventh spots in most lineups were a little bit interchangeable, with maybe some platoons or matchup-based decisions being made by the manager. The eighth and ninth spots were also interchangeable to a degree, and some American League managers would incorporate a leadoff type of hitter into the ninth spot. Back in the day, the bottom two in the order were pretty much average everyday players who were very good defenders. When someone at the top of the order did get a day off, it was common for a bottom-of-the-order guy to move up in the lineup to replace him.

Lineups were built around familiarities, and each spot in the order came with its own job description to a degree. Everything revolved around a team concept in which everyone had a job to do. Productive outs, two-strike approaches, sacrifice bunts, and hit-and-runs were required of some of the spots in the order, and these hitters knew and delivered what was expected of them. This expectation was handed down by the manager and reinforced every day by the coaching staff. There was never an individual approach outside of the team concept; any individuals who had an "I'm gonna get mine" approach were doing that because it was part of their job based on the manager's philosophy. Albert Belle, who in the mid-nineties was one of the game's premier sluggers, is a prime example of this kind of player. When I joined the Cleveland Indians at the end of 1995 and became a teammate of Albert's, I saw first-hand that when he was getting his, it also meant that the team was winning games. Albert hit 52 doubles and 50 home runs in just 143 games that strike-shortened season, but part of Albert being Albert meant leaving him alone from 4 to 10 pm each night.

Tinkering with the lineups has been done before. Tony LaRussa, the winningest manager in the modern era, should get more credit for the innovation of hitting the pitcher eighth and a position player ninth. He did this with the thought that the nine-hole hitter had a better chance of getting on base as the batting order was turning over. This also provided LaRussa with the ability to maybe get a pinch hitter in the game a few more times during the season. That thought comes from the idea that every spot in the order gets roughly fifteen to twenty more plate appearances compared to the spot behind it, meaning if the leadoff guy has 750 PAs, the two spot in the order will have around 735, and so on down the line.

•   •   •

Tony LaRussa, the winningest manager in the modern era, should get more credit for the innovation of hitting the pitcher eighth and a position player ninth.

Joe Maddon also did some tinkering of his own as the 2015 Cubs would sometimes hit shortstop Addison Russell in the nine spot, and he took it a little bit further by putting Kris Bryant in the two hole. Soon, other teams started following suit: The Blue Jays started batting their reigning MVP, Josh Donaldson, in the two spot. The Angels and Pirates did the same thing with Mike Trout and Andrew McCutchen, respectively, and in 2017, when then rookie Aaron Judge got hot, the Yankees and Joe Girardi batted him second as well. Christian Yelich, the 2018 National League MVP, and Mike Trout are now the poster boys for the modern-day lineup in which the team's best hitter hits second.

The lineups in today's game don't look like the ones from years past. I'm sure there are some mathematical reasons for the changes in teams' lineup configuration, and of course it's my job to question what those reasons are compared to baseball common sense. Having your best hitter hitting a spot or two higher in the lineup will get that hitter a few more plate appearances over the course of the year, but will those extra fifteen to twenty plate appearances put your team in a better position to score more runs? The theory of having my best get to home plate a few more times seems sound in the world where one plus one equals two, but I believe there are just too many variables at play for anyone to say, definitively, that it helps win more baseball games. If my best hitter plays every day, he will get 162 first-inning plate appearances batting in the two or three hole. In the two hole, he has only one hitter in front of him with a chance to get on base; in the three hole, he increases his chances to hit in the first inning with someone on base. Do the extra plate appearances coming to my best hitter batting second outweigh the first inning plate appearances he'd have with more men on base over the course of the year? Since I asked the question, you know which direction I'm leaning.

The production the Milwaukee Brewers have been getting
out of Christian Yelich in the two hole has been extraordinary, but
might he be even more productive hitting third or fourth in the lineup?

It's tough to argue with the numbers that Mike Trout and Christian Yelich are putting up now and have put up in the past. I believe their numbers could and should be even better than what they are, though. This is not an indictment of Trout or Yelich but rather an indictment of where their clubs hit them in the batting order. Individually, I don't think they can do any more than what they are doing right now. Circumstantially, the clubs need to put them in better situations. By the 2019 all-star break Yelich was sitting on thirty-one homers with twenty of those being solo.

Mike Trout had twenty-eight bombs at the break and sixteen of those were solos. Like I said, I don't think they can do any more, but if they batted a spot or two lower in the lineup with some guys in front of them who could get on base, it stands to reason that they might gain a few more multiple run homers under their belts. Can either or both of them win another MVP while hitting in the two hole? Yes, but is that really the best spot in the lineup for them to be in? I don't think it is. To take it a bit further, let's take a look at the total plate appearances among the major league's RBI leaders in 2019 through August 31st (Trout and Yelich both went on the Injured List in September):

## PLATE APPEARANCES WITH MEN ON BASE AMONG 2019 MLB RBI LEADERS THROUGH AUGUST 31ST

| | RBI | PA w/ Men On | Primary Batting Position |
|---|---|---|---|
| Josh Bell (PIT) | 109 | 292 | 4th |
| Freddie Freeman (ATL) | 109 | 281 | 3rd |
| Anthony Rendon (WSH) | 109 | 283 | 3rd |
| José Abreu (CWS) | 104 | 301 | 3rd |
| Cody Bellinger (LAD) | 101 | 296 | 4th |
| Pete Alonso (NYM) | 101 | 278 | 2nd |
| Mike Trout (LAA) | 101 | 254 | 2nd |
| Christian Yelich (MIL) | 89 | 238 | 2nd |

Yes, RBIs matter to me and when I look at the possibility of having Trout and Yelich getting a few more at bats with men on base, it's something I'd like to see happen. It's not even about having runners in scoring position; it's about having traffic on ahead of these guys that could make a difference. Through August 31st, Trout had 254 plate appearances with runners on base, thirty-eight fewer than the RBI leader, Josh Bell. With 238, Yelich was fifty-four plate appearances behind the leader in the same category.

Let's play a little game involving some math and probability. It involves the first three hitters in a team's lineup and the first inning of every game. This scenario also plays out every time during the year that the nine spot in the order makes the last out of an inning.

**Hitter A = .350 OBP**

**Hitter B = .350 OBP**

**Hitter X = Best Hitter**

1. Hitter A
2. Hitter X

Hitter X has a chance to hit with Hitter A on base 35 percent of the time or hit with the bases empty 65 percent of the time.

1. Hitter A
2. Hitter B
3. Hitter X

Hitter X has a chance to hit with at least one guy on base and sometimes two guys on base 57.25 percent of the time or hit with the bases empty 42.25 percent of the time.

This is math in a vacuum with a few assumptions being made. I know and have been pointing out in this book that one plus one doesn't always equal two in the baseball world and will acknowledge that these numbers are not exact when it comes to this exercise.

Some examples that do not enter into the math:

- Hitter A could hit a HR, and it would count on his OBP but he wouldn't be on base.
- Hitter A could walk and get picked off first.
- Hitter B could hit into a double play.
- Hitter B could hit a two-run home run and clear the bases.
- Fielder's choices or reaching base via error also does not enter into the math here. In these two cases, you can reach base without your on-base percentage going up.

I know from my experience and understanding of the game that these examples or similar ones pop up from time to time, but they really don't mess with the premise that having two guys capable of getting on base in front of my best hitter to start every game gives him the best chance to do damage in the first inning. If the object of the game is to score more runs than your opponent does, it should stand to reason that your best hitter be put in a position to maximize his talents. Scoring more runs or providing someone with the opportunity to drive in more runs makes sense, especially if that someone is your best. Individual numbers are great and having the highest OPS is great as well, but is this really helping the team score or drive in the most runs it can?

Hitting your best hitter third in the lineup guarantees him a plate appearance in the first inning and also increases the chance of hitting with a runner on base in that first inning. So for the way this exercise is laid out, the fifteen to twenty extra plate appearances that might be given to the two hitter in the lineup over the course of the year along with the 35 percent chance of having a runner on base in front of him in the first inning should not outweigh the eighty or ninety plate appearances that the three hole hitter will get with a man or two on base in the first inning alone.

The four-hole hitter is not guaranteed an at bat in the first inning, but if he does it will always be with a runner on base. Scoring first in a game goes hand-in-hand with winning, as teams that have scored first have won 67% of their games over the past five years. Obviously, scoring in the first inning is the best way to score first. Scoring multiple runs in the first inning is even better. I'm not trying to force every team to hit their best guy third. I am strongly suggesting, however, that it might be a really good idea. I realize some teams have a much more balanced or talented offense and they can do a little more tinkering than some other teams can.

## MLB SCORING FIRST RUN OF THE GAME

|  | W | L | PCT |
|---|---|---|---|
| 2019 | 1499 | 754 | .665 |
| 2018 | 1630 | 801 | .671 |
| 2017 | 1574 | 856 | .648 |
| 2016 | 1587 | 840 | .654 |
| 2015 | 1702 | 727 | .701 |

One more time, though I will be accused of cherry picking:
2017 World Baseball Classic winner: United States
Third hitter: Christian Yelich
Manager: Jim Leyland

Just saying.

# CHAPTER 23

# WEATHER AND BASEBALL

Sometimes you win, sometimes you lose, and sometimes you get rained out. In the early days of baseball, games would be played, clouds would roll in, and it would rain. When it rained hard enough, field conditions deteriorated, play was hampered, and the game was halted. If the field being played on had a tarp, it was applied. The waiting game would start and when it stopped raining, the field would get worked on a bit and play would resume if possible. If the field took on too much water, the powers that be would get together and postpone the game. The decision to play or cancel weather-affected games in yesteryear were made by people using common sense and judgment. In today's game, these decisions are dictated by weathermen. And while relying on science is, generally speaking, a better way to make an informed decision, there have been games in recent years that have been delayed for hours and even postponed without any precipitation falling because the forecast was inaccurate.

Weather has played a part in baseball since the game's earliest days. Better field construction, professional grounds crews, artificial turf, domes, and retractable roofs have all come into play over the years and have combined to allow the sport to continue with minimal delays and cancelations. But even with all the new technology and interactive weather-radar applications now at our disposal, Mother Nature has still won a few showdowns with baseball. She has made it snow in some northern cities like Minneapolis, Detroit, and Cleveland early on in the baseball season and she has sent some wintry temperatures into the playoffs and World Series. She also quite famously sent an earthquake to the 1989 World Series between Oakland and San Francisco and less famously sent a swarm of bees to San Diego, which delayed a 2009 Padres-Astros game by nearly an hour. Today's game has its new experts and with advances in technology and the rise of twenty-four-hour weather coverage, weather now has its own new crew of experts as well.

Some weather reporters and meteorologists have played a part in spreading the term *polar vortex*. It's a catchy thing to say; it rolls right off the tongue and I think when people hear it, they assume that whoever said it must know what they're talking about.

Below is from a 2014 ABC news story:

The polar vortex is real, and the meteorological community has known about it and used the term for decades. It is an almost always-present upper-level circulation that hangs out over the poles. It is not at the surface and is not related to every push of cold air.

During the first week of January 2014, the polar jet stream was kinked enough to build a large ridge in the west and allow a lobe of the polar vortex to slip into Canada, greatly influencing the air that set records in the northern plains and Great Lakes.

This has happened before, and for longer periods of time, such as in the late 1970s, but the term polar vortex did not get picked up back then by the general population.

Since January 2014, the term polar vortex has been used—and abused.

If we called every push of cold air the *polar vortex* it would lose its meaning and not be accurate.

My takeaway from the above news story is very similar to my take on how some people use certain terms in baseball. Just because something might sound good doesn't necessarily mean it's true. And using a fancy term doesn't necessarily make the speaker smarter or even correct when they use it. Naming something or making up a name for something seems way more important to some than understanding what the "something" actually is. When it's cold outside, the people who live in the Great Lakes region know. They don't need a weatherman to tell them what they can see for themselves by stepping out onto their porch.

"When it rains, it pours" is a well-worn saying that describes a domino-like situation that usually goes from bad to worse. This phrase ties into baseball as well as any other sport. It can apply to an individual game in which things are falling apart, or it can refer to a team that might be going through a rough week of injuries. In most cases, if not all, the ship eventually gets righted and things start looking up. In baseball, we now might be in the *pouring* phase of the phrase as all these new terms and stats are coming down on the game all at once. This, too, will run its course. The rain will slow, the clearing will start, and the sun will make its way out again. This sport has weathered many storms before and has emerged, once the clouds cleared, stronger for it.

# CHAPTER 24

# PHRASES
# OF THE GAME

The new school is trying to corner the market on naming these new-look statistics with catchy acronyms. I'm not sure if they're completely to blame for some of the terms or phrases in today's game or if there is a bit of collaboration going on. I've stated many times that there seems to be a need to measure everything in the game nowadays. Well now there seems to be a need to name everything, too, even if the thing being named has existed for years under a much simpler term. In some cases these new names are being thrown out there as a matter of fact, with no explanation, leaving those on the receiving end scratching their heads. I've had many people ask me, "What does this mean?" when referring to some of these new names or terms. I explain to the best of my ability, but I'm not exactly sure on all of them. I have a good idea on quite a few, but the meanings of some leave me speculating as well.

Let's look at some of the new names and terms that are being used around the game.

**Good bat-to-ball skills** refers to a good hitter. I guess it holds true since you clearly must have good bat-to-ball skills in order to hit. This is trying to replace the idea of "He can hit." Members of the old school would say that when referring to a guy who consistently hit stuff hard and was year over year a .280 hitter or above. He didn't strike out a lot, he didn't swing at too many bad pitches, and two-out knocks with runners in scoring position seemed to be a big part of his resume as well.

**Control the strike zone** refers to a hitter's ability not to chase pitches; I'm taking an educated guess on this one. It could also be a batter hitting his strikes rather than the pitcher's strikes early in the count. This is also trying to replace "He can hit" or "He has a good eye."

**Winning the battle of the strike zone** refers both to the hitters controlling the strike zone and to pitchers throwing strikes. This might sound better than "Get a good pitch and hit it" or "Strike one is the best pitch in baseball," but it is exactly what even the oldest of old schoolers would say.

**Spin it** refers to today's breaking balls in a variety of ways. "He can really spin it" is being applied to a guy with a very high spin rate on his curve ball. "He is spinning it more than ever" is used for a guy throwing more hooks than before. In today's game there is a need to spin it, so you've got me on this one.

**Converting ground balls into outs** refers to how effective the overshift is working. "We are doing a good job at converting ground balls into outs." This is dealing with a subset of a larger picture, and a little "spinning" might be going on here as well. Visit the overshift chapter again, please.

**80 hit tool** refers to a can't-miss hitter using the grading system used by scouts based off the 20–80 scale. The Blue Jays' Vladimir Guerrero Jr. carried this rating throughout his minor league days. This one has been around a long time but is now used as a punch line, and it's assumed that everyone knows what it means.

The Blue Jays' Vladimir Guerrero, Jr., pictured here as a minor leaguer, was one of the most highly rated prospects in recent years.

**Plus-plus** refers to well above average or excellent. Like the above, scouts would use "plus" as an adjective for a player. "He is a plus runner" means he is above average. "He is a plus-plus runner" means he is well above average—maybe even excellent. In most cases, the plus-plus refers to certain pitches in a pitcher's repertoire.

**Barrels** is a new stat that revolves around the idea that if a ball is hit and something happens that leads to something that then leads to something else, it is a barrel. According to MLB.com, a barrel is defined as "a well-struck ball where the combination of exit velocity and launch angle generally leads to a minimum .500 batting average and 1.500 slugging percentage." Furthermore, *The Hardball Times* says that the barrel zone "starts at an exit velocity of ninety-eight mph with a launch angle between twenty-six and thirty degrees, and then extends outwards." There are a lot of qualifiers for this one and we could also just look at the extra base hit leaders and pretty much see the same names on both leaderboards.

**Exit velocity** refers to how hard the ball comes off the bat when it's hit. It is one of the more frequently used terms and is a legitimate measurement. We have established that a home run is usually hit at 100 MPH or more. When a home run is hit, there seems to be an obligatory mention of the exit velocity, which bothers me because it seems to take the place of the particulars involved in actually hitting the home run. It's the easy way out for someone to talk about a specific home run without knowing how or why it happened.

**High leverage situation** refers to a team's best pitchers facing key hitters at a crucial part of the game. This one's a moving target, as the crucial part of the game could occur at any time. But if a team is leading 3–0 in the seventh inning and they're about to face the heart of their opponent's order, that's a high-leverage situation that calls for the closer or the "best" of the bullpen to be in the game. This is not my way of thinking, but that's how the term is used.

**Bull-penning** refers to using many relievers during a game. A new school baseball manager may have his starter go just three or four innings and then have a second pitcher go three innings before replacing him with two other relievers to finish the game. If an old school baseball manager uses three relievers for one inning each after his starter went six, I don't consider that bull-penning, especially if the relievers are fulfilling prescribed roles like setup man and closer. Four total pitchers are used in both examples, but the second example is straight out of the old school handbook and therefore thought to be outdated by those in the new school.

**Hit probability** refers to the chance of a batted ball being a hit depending on several factors. I prefer to think that if it's a hit, it had a 100 percent chance of being a hit. Bloopers, Texas leaguers, and seeing-eye ground ball knocks included. A ball finding its way around the Pesky Pole in Boston could have a 5 percent chance of being a hit even though it went in the seats for a home run.

**Catch probability** refers to the chance of a batted ball being caught by an outfielder depending on several factors. I prefer to think that if it's caught, it had 100 percent chance of being caught. The outfield walls or sidewalls near foul lines are not part of the equation of this stat yet, so a well-timed leap while robbing a homer and tumbling over a wall could have a 90 percent catch probability.

**Surplus value** refers to a player's value above and beyond what his salary is buying. If a guy making $1 million a year posts a WAR of 4 and, depending on who you talk to, the value of 1 WAR is $5–7 million, the player in theory is worth $20–28 million. Since this player only got paid $1 million, he would have a surplus value between $19–27 million. This surplus value goes in no one's pocket and you already know how I feel about WAR.

**Intrinsic pitch value** refers to what any one pitch actually does. The read on this one could be one of the most complicated reads we will ever have. The short version: It's about the movement of a pitch and placing a value on that movement. Results are not involved in this value, so a nasty slider that gets a high value could be hit for a game winner.

These are just a few of the highly used terms that are being thrown out there in game broadcasts and studio shows these days. Newspapers and websites are littered with articles that employ some of these phrases and terms as well. Statistics, tables, and graphs are being fabricated to support them. These are the ones that I could most accurately address and that most irk me when I hear them. They also don't bug me enough or carry enough weight for me to address in a standalone chapter. There are many, many more terms and stats being used that I can't offer any helpful clarification on what they're about, though. I use baseball common sense as my guide and looking up and trying to get through fragments of some of these definitions leaves me confused and my head hurting.

If I'm to play the rename game, I'll choose to have a little innocent fun. Dinger, big fly, tater, bomb, big ball, bridge, tank, yard, and oppo taco are a few entertaining euphemisms for the home run. A base hit can go by rocket, laser, tracer, or knock, while the bloop hit might be called a gork, thang, bleeder, or even a duck snort. Pitches can have their colorful names too. Heater, cheese, gas, butter, naked heat, petrol, pellet, and aspirin are all words that are used to describe a fastball. The curveball over time has been called a hook, overhand yellow hammer, hammer, Uncle Charlie, Lord Charles, snapdragon, 12–6, and a yacker. The two-seam fastball has been described as a bowling ball, a good change is said to act like a dead fish, and a hanging slider is sometimes known as a cement mixer. These are perfect names and descriptions to an old school baseball guy.

Finding different ways to say things isn't a problem. In teaching baseball, I've found that saying something differently might allow the student to grasp an idea a little easier. The terms *inside-out swing* and *staying inside the baseball* basically describe the same idea, the same way *casting your swing* and *surrounding the baseball* do. One term may resonate with a hitter more than another.

Saying things slightly differently is one thing, but overloading something with complicated ideas is a completely different monster. Our first pillar in the Ripken Way is keeping it simple; that doesn't mean lack of substance in any way. I can get as deep as you want to go on a baseball field, and I can do it with simple gestures, terms, and phrases.

# CHAPTER 25

# THE FUTURE

No one truly knows what the future will bring. In baseball terms, though, the immediate future lies with the players and the owners' ability to keep the peace as far as the collective bargaining agreement goes. Baseball has enjoyed labor peace since 1995, and the current CBA expires at the end of 2020. Hopefully the owners and players can work through some of their issues and get something done before that. Work stoppages have happened before with both sides being the heavy; the owner's tool is a lockout and the players use the strike. In either case, no one really wins. If one side sort of wins, that's another story. I'd like to think that without a couple of those work stoppages the game would be just as good as it is right now, but who knows for sure? Maybe the past labor unrest was actually worth the growing pains. I don't want to see us test that theory with another work stoppage, though. Both sides need to take a hard look at what's at stake should another work stoppage occur due to labor issues. The money is certainly there for both sides and the game is still good, so I urge both sides to figure it out and get something done.

Assuming a new CBA gets done, baseball is in a very good place and the future of the game looks bright. In my opinion it's the best sport going, and my hope for the game revolves around what's already great about it. The young talent on display is tremendous and we should be celebrating this more than anything else. I do not see as much wrong with this game as others do. I hear more conversations about how the game is changing and there is a need for more changes, but if I put on some noise-canceling headphones and watch the game, I see a game that looks really familiar to me for the most part. The team that plays *baseball* better than the other team wins the game. This holds true today just as it did back in the day.

Batting your best hitter in the two hole and beginning a game not with a true starting pitcher but an opener are a couple of things the new school has introduced, but the game being played looks the same. The opener might throw just the first inning but he pitches from the same mound that everyone else pitches from and has to get hitters out the same way too. The hitter batting in the two hole may be your team's best hitter, but he's still one of nine hitters in the batting order. You're still pitching and hitting and throwing and catching the baseball and, despite some innovations, pretty much everything in the game today has been done before. I believe the designated hitter being used in the American League (which should soon be used in the National League), the interleague games, and the wild card were the last firsts in the game that have stood the test of time. Will the opener and the best hitter batting second in the lineup hold up to that standard? We will see; only time will tell.

Ideas have been introduced throughout baseball's history that have worked well and remained a part of the game. There have also been ideas that have worked all right and had a place in the game for a while, and ideas that didn't work so well and didn't last long at all. Innovation, ideas, and experimentation have always been a part of the game, and it's what has enabled baseball both to endure and evolve. Part of being smart is understanding what works and what doesn't while also understanding that a good idea in theory sometimes doesn't quite work in reality. Every few years someone comes up with a better way to play the game, only to see that better way revert back to the way the game was being played before. Tweaking the rules a bit to try and make the game incrementally better, accounting for the ever-improving skillsets of the players, and looking at safety while putting rules into place to keep the talent of the game healthy should always be priorities of Major League Baseball. When something has been around as long as baseball has, it gets harder to achieve firsts. Sometimes the next edition of something has a chance to work, but it truly needs to be the next edition and not just a repeat of an idea that didn't work in the first place.

Analytics will always be a part of this game moving forward because it has always been a part of this game. Sabermetrics are going be a part of this game moving forward as well, but I think they will play a small part because the number of loyal users and promoters of these somewhat predictive stats is small. The current wave of stats such as Defensive Runs Saved (DRS), Weighted On-Base Average (wOBA), Weighted Runs Created Plus (wRC+), and Outs Above Average (OAA) will no doubt take on adjustments to their definitions or give way to new letter combinations as their creators search for the next best thing. I say this with complete certainty because Fielding Independent Pitching (FIP) and Ultimate Zone Rating (UZR) are a couple of the early, overused terms that have already been quieted by either lack of meaning or replaced by a somewhat better version, or both. Some of these fancy acronyms and abbreviations probably took longer to name than they were actually used.

Old school baseball numbers are real and have been applied to players such as Babe Ruth, Henry Aaron, Mickey Mantle, Ted Williams, Roberto Clemente, Sandy Koufax, Bob Gibson, Nolan Ryan, Willie Mays, and Pete Rose. The numbers that these guys put up meant something in baseball and they still should. Going back through the years and having the sabermetric crew try to put an adjusted spin on these real numbers is hard for me to grasp. In order to adjust these numbers, they must plug the actual numbers into their formulas. How long has an RBI been an RBI, a run a run, a hit a hit, an error an error, a win a win or a strikeout a strikeout? These numbers provide a few questions for *some* and I understand that, but they are questioned far less by far fewer people than the newfangled numbers are. These are numbers that say a lot and have said a lot over the years, and if you know what you're looking for they can be quite informative. If you go to any of the websites promoting sabermetric statistics and spend ten minutes browsing the plethora of stats, you will leave the site more confused than you were before you looked them up. Don't take my word for it; go check it out.

The new versus the old and the combination of the new and old will be ongoing discussions as baseball moves forward. I'm sure the conversation will grow even larger on the outside of the game in the future, just as I believe it's larger now on the outside than the inside. There are definitely more numbers being looked at in front offices in today's game, but I'm not even close to being convinced that all those numbers make it down to or are used by the players. The players playing the game *are* the game. It's been that way since the game started. The old school has always used numbers or analytics of some sort to better itself. The old school also has legitimate baseball experience to draw from that can only be obtained by being a part of or playing the game at the highest level. These experiences have been accumulated over many years and cannot be taken for granted or assumed not to matter. The new school has forged out a nice spot in the game, and as I've stated earlier in this book, it does bring something to the table. I just hope the really smart people in the game now understand who the true baseball people are in their organizations. The game has always had trends that come and go, and the new school may be one of them. The old school is capable of learning more, but there are only so many numbers needed in playing this game, and the group that has played the game and been around the game the longest are the ones most qualified to make that call.

The new and the old can and should coexist moving forward. I'll be here watching as they do. I'll give credit where credit is due, but I will also be watching the baseball being played and identifying the pure reasons driving both success and failure. There are smart people in front offices today just as there were smart people in front offices back in the day. The teams that succeed in the future will be the ones with the outside-of-the-box front office thinkers doing their thing and then turning over the information to the more inside-of-the-box thinkers in the clubhouse. I guarantee that the box in the clubhouse will get bigger if the information being handed down is useful. Front offices working with managers, not running roughshod over them, will be the key to success moving forward. If this happens, all will be good and the game will continue to look the same. If it doesn't, it will show and it will prove to be unsuccessful. The blame for that should go upstairs. When blame is assigned, moves are made, and then who knows? Those moves might bring back some old school front office executives, and the game will once again be talked about the way it once was. Baseball has been very cyclical over the years and, for better or worse, it's certainly had its share of trends. But as long as there are old school baseball men in the game, the sport will be in good hands.

## ACKNOWLEDGMENTS

A number of people contributed, directly and indirectly, to making this book a reality.

Thanks, Mom and Dad, for being you and for always pushing the right buttons. Thanks, Mom, for being both you and Dad when he wasn't around. You two always gave me a chance.

Thanks to my siblings, Elly, Cal, and Fred, who have all had a part in shaping me into who I am.

Thanks to all the coaches and teammates I've had along the way.

Thanks to the men and women working behind the scenes at Major League Baseball Network, especially in the content, editing, and research areas.

Thanks to Moses Massena, who for the past decade has been a great resource and sounding board for my thoughts and ideas. You were a big key in getting my thoughts onto paper for this book and a big part of this project from the very beginning.

Thanks to John Maroon of Maroon PR and the team at Diversion Books—Scott Waxman, Mark Weinstein, and Emily Hillebrand—for their contributions on this book's behalf. You guys have been great.

Thank you.

**BILL RIPKEN,** a former twelve-year major league veteran, is a studio analyst appearing across MLB Network's programming, including the Emmy Award–winning flagship studio show *MLB Tonight*. A three-time sports Emmy nominee, he captured the award for Outstanding Studio Analyst in 2016.

Ripken began his playing career with the Baltimore Orioles in 1987 under the direction of his father, Cal Ripken Sr., and alongside his legendary brother, Cal Ripken Jr. This marked the first and only time in Major League Baseball history that a father simultaneously managed two of his sons. After playing for Baltimore through 1992 and again in 1996, Ripken played for the Texas Rangers (1993–1994 and 1997), Cleveland Indians (1995), and Detroit Tigers (1998). In 1988, Ripken finished second among American League second basemen in double plays turned with 110 and his .9927 fielding percentage in 1992 led all Major League second baseman that season. Ripken led the Orioles in hitting with a .291 average and was tied for first on the team with twenty-eight doubles in 1990.

In the spring of 2002, Ripken was honored for his achievements with an induction into the Maryland Sports Hall of Fame. In 2009 Ripken served as first base coach for team USA at the World Baseball Classic.

After his playing career, Bill formed Ripken Baseball with his brother Cal. The pillar of the youth side of this business is hosting baseball and softball tournaments at four premier destinations. Ripken Baseball owns or operates facilities in Aberdeen Maryland, Myrtle Beach, South Carolina, Pigeon Forge, Tennessee, and Orlando, Florida, at Disney World. Ripken Professional Baseball owns and operates the Aberdeen IronBirds, a Class A (New York Penn League) affiliate of the Baltimore Orioles.

In 2001 Bill and Cal established The Cal Ripken Sr. Foundation, in memory of the family's patriarch. The foundation is a 501(c)(3) non-profit organization, working throughout the country with Boys & Girls Clubs, P.A.L. centers, the United States Department of Justice, the United States Marshals Service, local law enforcement groups, inner-city schools, and other youth-serving organizations supporting programs in America's most distressed communities.

Ripken and his wife of thirty-plus years, Candace, have four children: Miranda, Anna, Reese, and Jack.

Associated Press; Eric Christian Smith / AP / Associated Press; AP / Associated Press; LM Otero / AP / Associated Press; Gregory Bull / AP / Associated Press; Eric Christian Smith / AP / Associated Press; Patrick Semansky / AP / Associated Press; Andrew Harnik / AP / Associated Press; David Dermer / FR171035 / Associated Press; Robert Beck / SPTSW / Associated Press; Robert Beck / SPTSW / Associated Press; Morry Gash / AP / Associated Press

Photos on pages xxix, 86, 108 appear courtesy of MLB Network

# INDEX

Aaron, Henry Louis ("Hank"), 192
Aberdeen Ironbirds (Class A), 198
Abreu, José, 173
acronyms, naming/defining. *See also* "new school" names/terms
   about: "new"/"old" school, xxi, xxviii; what will be next new, 191
   bWAR (Baseball-Reference stat), 70–71
   DRS (Defensive Runs Saved), 79–85
   ERA (Earned Run Average), 47–53
   fWAR (FanGraphs stat), 70–71
   OAA (Outs Above Average), 101, 191
   OBP (On-Base Percentage), 61–65
   OPS (On-Base Plus Slugging), 121–126
   OPS+ (weighted On-Base Plus Slugging), 124
   RBI (Runs Batted In), 117–120
   SLG (Slugging Percentage), 31, 123–124
   UZR (Ultimate Zone Rating), 81, 83, 122
   WAR (Wins Above Replacement), 67–68
   wOBA (Weighted On-Base Average), 124, 191
   wRC+ (Weighted Runs Created Plus), 120, 191
   ZE (Zone Evaluation), 108
Acuna, Ronald, Jr., 139
Ahmed, Nick, 80
Alonso, Pete, 173

Altuve, José, xxii, 109, 110
Arenado, Nolan, 83, 117–118
Arizona Diamondbacks, xxii, 98
*The Athletic* (sports website), xiii
Atlanta Braves, xix, xxiii, 25, 87, 89, 90
Australia, professional baseball in, 129
automated strike zone ("robo-umps"), 109–111, 115
Avery, Steve, xxiii

Bader, Harrison, 80
Báez, Javier, 31, 32
Balboni, Steve, 88
ball in the dirt, 22, 23, 27, 80–81, 86
*Baltimore (Evening) Sun*, xii
Baltimore Orioles
   Bill Ripken playing career, xii, 88, 150, 197–198
   Cal, Sr. as player, manager and coach, 1–9, 197
   "The Oriole Way," 11
"barrels," 184
baseball common sense, using, xv–xxvii, 9, 12, 79, 84, 102, 143, 145, 161, 171
baseball draft, xvii, 6, 32, 143–144, 145
Baseball Writers of America, 1
Baseball-Reference.com, 69–71
batting average, 61–65, 70–73, 84–85, 92–95, 99, 104, 117–119, 121–124, 184
   pitchers vs. designated hitters, 130

batting order, 132, 163, 166, 169, 172, 190
batting stance, set-up and swing, 14–17, 33, 35. *See also* launch angle
Baylor, Don, 8
Belanger, Mark, 8
Bell, Josh, 33–37, 173–174
Belle, Anthony, xxiii
Bellinger, Cody, xxiv, 33, 95, 123, 173
Belt, Brandon, xxiv
bench players, 150–151
Benintendi, Andrew, xxiv
Betts, Mookie, xxiv, 31, 75, 80
Bill's Blackboard, xxix, 86, 108
Bogaerts, Xander, xxiv
Boggs, Wade, 25
Bonds, Barry, 121, 164–167
Boston Red Sox, xxiv, 74–75, 77, 88–89
Bradley, Jackie, Jr., xxiv, 69
Braun, Ryan, 71
Bregman, Alex, xxii, 83–84, 100, 123
Broxton, Keon, 69
Bryant, Kris, 117–118, 148–149, 171
Buehler, Walker, xxiv
bullpen/bullpen games, xviii, 47, 160–161, 185
"bull-penning," 185
Bumbry, Al, 8
Bumgarner, Madison, xxiv
bunts/bunting, 29, 131, 132, 163–166, 169
Buxton, Byron, 69
bWAR (Baseball-Reference stats), 70–71

Cabell, Enos, 7, 8
Cain, Lorenzo, xxiv, 80
Cain, Matt, xxiv
The Cal Ripken Sr. Foundation, 12, 198
Canó, Robinson, 87–88
Carapazza, Vic, 113
Carpenter, Matt, 95

Carpenter, Ruly, 128–129
Casey, Sean, 30
Cashman, Brian, xx
"catch probability," 185–186
Cespedes, Yoenis, 75–77
Chamberlain, Wes, 152
Chance, Dean, 8
Chapman, Matt, 80, 82–83
Chicago Cubs, 26, 31–32, 63–64, 71–72, 89–91, 94, 148–149, 171
Chicago White Sox, 26
Clemens, Roger, 51
Clemente, Roberto, 192
Cleveland Indians, xxiii, 169, 178, 197
Clevinger, Mike, 43
coaches/coaching. *See also* manager(s)
  Bill Ripken as, xv–xvi, 198
  Cal, Sr. as, xii, xvi, 1–9
  impact of the "new school" on, xx–xxi
  keeping it simple, 13–14
  maintaining an element of fun, 17–19
  recognizing player differences, 15–17
  role in team development, 136, 169
  role in Ripken experiment, 144–145
  teaching is part of, 14–15, 37–38
code of conduct (unwritten rules), 112, 153–157
Cole, Alex, 165
Cole, Gerrit, xxii, 42
collective bargaining agreement (CBA), 189–190
"control the strike zone," 182
"converting ground balls into outs," 182–183
Cora, Alex, xx
Correa, Carlos, xxii, 69, 70
Cox, Bobby, xx
Crawford, Brandon, xxiv

Cruz, Nelson, 123, 130
Cy Young Award, 23, 26, 49–51, 58–59

Dalton, Harry, 4
d'Arnaud, Travis, 99
Davis, Gerry, 113
DeCinces, Doug, 8
defense/defensive positioning, 71, 81, 87–100, 102–103, 107, 137–138, 152, 160–162
Defensive Runs Saved (DRS)
  as replacement for errors, 101
  common sense, going against, 79
  doesn't really mean anything, 84–85
  examples/player ranking, 80
  misleading nature of, 80–83
  problems with the statistic, 83–85, 191
Defensive Wins Above Replacement (DWAR), 101
deGrom, Jacob, 23, 49–50
DeJong, Paul, 33
designated hitters, 127–133
Detroit Tigers, 198
Diaz, Laz, 113
Dombrowski, Dave, xx
double plays, xvi, 13, 81, 150, 175, 198
Doubleday, Abner, 97
Drake, Rob, 113
Duda, Lucas, 99
Dykstra, Lenny, 152

Earned Run Average (ERA), pitching and, 47–53, 75, 97
Etchebarren, Andy, 8
"80 hit tool," 183
Eisenrich, Jim, 152
ejections, 112, 154
Elias Sports Bureau, 70
Ellsbury, Jacoby, xxiv
errors
  attempts to replace, 101–102, 107
  defined, 104

determining what are, 104–105
fewer errors wins games, 102–103
"new school" view of, 81
taking care of the ball reduces, 106–107
"exit velocity," 184
expansion, xxv–xxix
experimentation, new ideas/rule changes, 115, 141–145. See also innovations

FanGraphs.com, 67, 70–71, 91–92
Fielding Independent Pitching (FIP), 191
Flanagan, Mike, 8, 12
Flowers, Tyler, 26
Freeman, Freddy, 95, 173
front office operations, xii, xix–xxi, 6–7, 136, 142, 192–193. See also managers
fundamentals, putting fun into the, 17–19
fWAR (FanGraphs stats), 70–71

Gehrig, Lou, 1, 166
Gibson, Bob, xxv, 192
Giles, Bill, 128–129
Glavine, Tom, xxiii
Gomes, Jonny, 75
Gonzalez, Carlos, 95
Gonzalez, Gio, 24
Gonzalez, Juan, 117, 166
"good bat-to-bat skills, 182
Gordon, Alex, xxiv
Grandal, Yasmani, 26, 27
Granderson, Curtis, 87–88, 99
Greinke, Zack, xxii, 23, 97–99
Grich, Bobby, 8
Griffey, Ken, Jr., 33

Hall of Fame. See National Baseball Hall of Fame
Harper, Bryce, 63–64, 117–118, 139
Herrera, Kelvin, xxiv
Heyward, Jason, 71–72
Hickox, Ed, 113

*The Hidden Game of Baseball*
  (Palmer), 122
"high leverage situation," 185
"hit probability," 185
hit-and-run, 163, 169
Holland, Greg, xxiv
Houston Astros, xxii, 23, 26, 53,
  83–84, 90, 100, 141
Hrbek, Ken, 88
Hriniak, Walt, 17

Incaviglia, Pete, 152
Inciarte, Ender, 80
innovations, new ways of playing,
  xxi, 169–170, 189–193. *See also*
  experimentation
Inside Edge, 91–93
International League (Triple-A), 129
"intrinsic pitch value," 186

Jansen, Kenley, xxiv
Japan, professional baseball in, 123,
  129
Jeter, Derek, xxiii, 85, 105, 139
Johnson, Randy, xxiv, 59
Jones, Andruw, xxiii
Jones, Chipper, xxiii, 139
Jones, JaCoby, 80
Judge, Aaron, 109, 110, 171
Justice, David, xxiii

Kansas City Royals, xxiv, 26, 76,
  90, 97
Kendrick, Howie, 99
Kershaw, Clayton, xxiv
Keuchel, Dallas, xxii
Kluber, Corey, 23, 43
Korea, professional baseball in, 70,
  129
Koufax, Sandy, 192
"K-zone," 23

Lau, Charlie, 17
launch angle ("exit angle"). *See also*
  batting stance, set-up and swing
  examples/player ranking, 31

importance of the swing, 32–34
misconceptions, 34–38 0
origins/meaning, 29–3
left-handed hitters, 32–33, 57, 59–60,
  87–95
left-handed pitchers, 109, 151
LeMahieu, D. J., 80
Lester, Jon, xxiv, 75–76
Libka, John, 113
Lincecum, Tim, xxiv
Lindor, Francisco, 69, 70, 80
lineup configuration
  batting order and, 163–168
  building on team concept, 169–171
  changes in today's game, 171–173
  plate appearances and, 173–176
Little, Will, 113
Livensparger, Shane, 113
Lopez, Javy, xxiii
Los Angeles Angels, 26
Los Angeles Dodgers, xxiv, 26, 33,
  97, 99
Lowrie, Jed, 69, 70
Lugo, Seth, 42
Luzinski, Greg, 128

Machado, Manny, 69, 70, 117–118,
  139
Maddon, Joe, 63, 87, 89, 91, 171
Maddux, Greg, 56–58, 60
Maldonado, Martin, 26
manager(s). *See also* coaches/
  coaching; front office operations
  Cal, Sr. as, xii, 1–9, 11
  game strategy and, 63, 131–132,
    164, 168–169
  Joe Maddon as, 63, 87, 91
  "new"/"old" school differences,
    xviii–xxi, 185
  role in team development, 136
  role in the Ripken experiment,
    144–145
  Tony LaRussa as, 169–170
  working with the front office, 193
Mantle, Mickey, 192
Maryland Sports Hall of Fame, 198

matchups/matchup statistics,
xvii–xviii, 49, 168
May, Ben, 113
Mays, Willie, Jr., 192
McCutchen, Andrew, 71, 171
McPhail, Lee, 4
Merrill, Durwood, 24
Mexico, professional baseball in, 129
Miami Marlins, 2, 90
Millwood, Kevin, xxiii
Milwaukee Brewers, 26, 27, 172
Moreland, Keith, 128
Morton, Charlie, xxiv, 43
Moustakas, Mike, xxiv
Murphy, Daniel, 99
Murray, Eddie, 8, 12, 117, 139, 166,
168

Nagy, Charles, xxiii
National Baseball Hall of Fame
Cal Ripken, Jr., 1
Lee McPhail, 4
"new school" baseball. *See also*
sabermetrics
bringing change to the game,
xii–xiii, xxii–xxv
comparison to "old school,"
xvii–xviii
creating/naming new terms,
181–187
differences in play, 34, 38, 62–65,
73, 91, 119, 137, 165–166, 190
finding balance with "old school,"
xix–xxi, xxviii–xxix, 102,
192–193
measured against an "old school"
control, 141–145
reliance on numbers alone,
104–105
what the future may being,
189–193
"new school" names/terms. *See also*
acronyms
about: creation of, 181; need for
common sense, 186–187
"barrels," 184

"bull-penning," 185
"catch probability," 185–186
"control the strike zone," 182
"converting ground balls into
outs," 182–183
"80 hit tool," 183
"exit velocity," 184
"good bat-to-bat skills, 182
"high leverage situation," 185
"hit probability," 185
"intrinsic pitch value," 186
"plus-plus," 184
"spin it," 182
"surplus value," 186
"winning the battle of the strike
zone," 182
New York Mets, 42, 49–50, 77, 90,
97–99
New York Yankees, xx, xxiii, 39,
67–68, 85, 87–88, 90, 109
Nola, Aaron, 42

Oakland Athletics, 51, 75–76
Ogea, Chad, xxiii
"old school" baseball. *See also* The
Ripken Way
balancing sabermetrics with, xi–xiii
baseball is still baseball, xv–xix
changes from the "new school"
revolution, xix–xxv
the coach is not a dictator, 15
expansion and dilution, xxv–xxix
what the future may being,
189–193
Olson, Matt, 80
On-Base Percentage (OBP), 61–65,
73, 174–175
On-Base Plus Slugging (OPS)
calculating the values, 122–123
examples/player ranking, 123,
151–152
making sense out of, 123–124, 126
usefulness of, 121–122, 175
"The Oriole Way," 11–12
Outs Above Average (OAA), 101,
191

overshifts
  considerations for using, 92–93
  hitters it hurts most, 94–95
  increased popularity of, 87–92
  working as a defensive unit,
    95–100

Pacific League (Triple-A), 129
Palmer, Jim, 8
Palmer, Pete, 122
Panik, Joe, xxiv
Papelbon, Jonathan, xxiv
Parcells, Bill, 159
Pederson, Joc, xxiv
Pedroia, Dustin, xxiv
Pettitte, Andy, xxiii
pitch count, 47
pitch framing
  ball control by pitcher and, 23–24
  catcher and, 21–22, 25–27
  hitter's ability for influencing,
    24–25
  role of the umpire in, 25
  score of the game and, 25
  stadium and fans as factor, 25
pitching wins
  evaluating a win-loss record,
    48–50
  in the end, wins matter, 51–53
  "new school" analytics and,
    47–48
Pittsburgh Pirates, 33–37, 128–129,
  164–167, 171
platooning, 151–152
player development, xix–xx, 4, 11–12,
  18, 138–140, 143–145
"plus-plus," 184
Posada, Jorge, xxiii
Posey, Buster, xxiv, 26, 71
positional versatility
  bench players, 150–151
  platooning, 151–152
  utility players, 147–149
Price, David, 42
productive outs, xv, 161, 169
Puig, Yasiel, xxiv

Pujols, Albert, 73–74, 78
putting the ball in play, xv, 94

rain-delayed games, 177–179
Ramirez, José, 69, 70
Ramirez, Manny, xxiii, 166
Reinbach, Mike, 7
relief specialization, 47
Rendon, Anthony, 123, 173
Reynolds, Mark, 69, 70, 130
right-handed hitters, 32–33, 59–60,
  90–91, 96, 151
Ripken, Anna, v, 198
Ripken, Calvin Edward, Jr. ("Cal")
  baseball IQ and experience, xii,
    15–16, 95–96, 105
  career accomplishments, 1, 15
  career statistics, 8–9, 105–106
  minor league career, 139
  photographs, 18, 114
  post-playing career, 198
Ripken, Calvin Edward, Sr. ("Cal"),
  1–9
  as epitome of "The Oriole Way,"
    11–12
  childhood and end of playing days,
    1–3
  death, 12
  manager in the minor leagues,
    3–8
  managing his sons, 8–9, 197
  photographs, xvi, 2, 5, 18, 114
  pillars of "The Ripken Way,"
    11–19
Ripken, Candace, v, 198
Ripken, Jack, v, 198
Ripken, Miranda, v, 198
Ripken, Oliver & Bill, 3
Ripken, Reese, v, 198
Ripken, William Oliver (Bill, "Billy
  the Kid")
  as part of the "old school," xi–xii
  baseball IQ and experience,
    xii–xiii, xv–xxix
  minor league career, 139–140
  MLB playing career, 9, 197–198

photographs, xxvii, xxix, 18, 86, 197
post-playing career, 198
proposing an "old school" experiment, 142–145
using Bill's Blackboard, xxix, 86, 108
Ripken Baseball (youth program), xv–xvi, 12, 198
Ripken Professional Baseball, 198
The Ripken Way (the 4 pillars)
  about: origins of, 11–12
  1. Keep It Simple, 12–14
  2. Explain the Why, 14–15
  3. Celebrate the Individual, 15–17
  4. Make It Fun, 17–19
Rivera, Mariano, xxiii
Rizzo, Anthony, 25, 94–95
"robo-umps" (automated strike zone), 109–111, 115
Rocker, John, xxiii
Romo, Sergio, xxiv
Rose, Pete, 192
Ross, Cody, 69, 70
rules/rulebook
  automated strike zone, 115
  changing the pitcher, 131
  designated hitter, 127–133
  hits and errors, 104
  making the last out at third, 136–137
  Ripken Baseball, 12–19
  strike zone, 109, 111
  tweaks to make the game better, 191
  unwritten code of conduct, 153–157
run differential, 159–162
Runs Batted In (RBI)
  how the runs are counted, 118–119
  lineup configuration and, 164–165, 173–176
  "new"/"old" school differences, 73, 117, 119–120, 192
  notable player counts, 9, 36–37, 62–63, 118, 123

Russo, Christopher ("Mad Dog"), 80
Ruth, George Herman ("Babe"), 192
Ryan, Nolan ("Big Tex"), 23, 24, 192
Ryu, Hyun-Jin, xxiv

sabermetrics. See also "new school" baseball
  balancing "old school" with, xi–xiii, 191–193
  batting average doesn't matter, 61–62
  common sense can work with, xv–xxix
  DRS concept is not reality, 83–85
  needing to name everything, 56–57
  OPS as a meaningful stat, 123–126
  WAR defined, 67, 77
  WAR differences in calculations, 70–71
sacrifice bunt, 166, 169
sacrifice fly, 99
salary cap, 142
Sale, Chris, 59–60
San Diego Padres, 26
San Francisco Giants, xxiv, 26, 42, 59, 76, 90, 167
Sanchez, Gary, 67–68
Sandoval, Pablo, xxiv
Scherzer, Max, 42, 50, 133, 172
Schuerholz, John, xx
scouts/scouting reports, xi, xii, xvii, xix, 95, 102, 144, 183–184
Seager, Corey, xxiv
Seattle Mariners, 26, 123
Severino, Luis, 39–40
Simmons, Andrelton, 80
Slugging Percentage (SLG), 31, 123, 124
Snell, Blake, 43
Soto, Juan, 33, 139–140
Spahn, Warren, 47, 48
"spin it," 182
spin rate
  as a diagnostic tool, 45
  breaking balls, 43
  curveballs, 42–43

spin rate (*cont.*)
  fastballs, 39–42
  meaning of, 39
  using combinations, 44–45
Springer, George, xxii
St. Louis Cardinals, xxv, 18, 22, 33
Stanton, Giancarlo, 69, 70
statistics. *See also* Defensive Runs
  Saved; Earned Run Average;
  Runs Batted In; Wins Above
  Replacement
  balancing "new"/"old"
    approaches, xii–xiii, xviii, xxv,
    192
  beginning of new, xi, xxi–xxii
  Cal, Jr. career, 8–9
  creating/naming "new," xxi, xxviii,
    181–187
  designated hitter, 128
  making an expert, xxviii
  need for new defensive play, 107
  run differential, 160–161
  things not measured by, 4, 25–26,
    102
Stewart, Dave, 51
Stratton, Chris, 42
strike zone
  automated/"robo-umps," 109–111,
    115
  defined, 109, 111
  evaluating umpires, 111–115
  expanding the size, 25, 64
  "new school" terms, 182
  pitch framing and, 21–27
strikeouts, xv, 37–38, 49, 94, 192
"surplus value," 186
Suzuki, Ichiro, 123–124
Swisher, Nick, 87–88

Tampa Bay Rays, xix, 26, 87–90,
  141
Tavárez, Julián, xxiii
Teherán, Julio, 24, 42
Teixeira, Mark, 87–88
Texas Rangers, 197
Thames, Eric, 70

Thomas, Frank, 25
Thome, Jim, xxiii, 30, 166
Thompson, Mitt, 152
Thorn, John, 122
Topps baseball cards, 122
Toronto Blue Jays, 90, 171, 183
Torre, Joe, xx
Trout, Mike, 25, 33, 62–63, 121–122,
  123, 125, 173–174
tunneling ("piping")
  analytics and the need to name
    everything, 56–57
  deception and, 58–59
  meaning of/term origins, 55–56
  as part of success in pitching,
    59–60
Turner, Justin, 99
two-strike approach, xv, 33, 80, 169

Ultimate Zone Rating (UZR), 81, 83,
  101, 122, 191
umpires
  automated/"robo-umps," 109–111,
    115
  calling balls and strikes, 21, 23–25
  evaluating performance, 26,
    111–115
  expanding the strike zone, 25
  player ejections, 112, 154
  standing behind the mound, 44
unwritten rules (code of conduct),
  112, 153–157
utility players, 147–152

Ventura, Yordano, xxiv
Verlander, Justin, xxii, 23, 43, 44,
  133
Votto, Joey, 24, 25, 71, 122

Walker, Tom, 7
walks vs. hits, 62–65, 99, 119,
  123–124
Washington Nationals, 53, 63–64,
  140
watering down the talent pool,
  xxv–xxix

weather/weather-delayed games, 177–179
Weaver, Earl, 5, 12, 166
Weighted On-Base Average (wOBA), 191
Weighted Runs Created Plus (wRC+), 120, 191
Welch, Bob, 51
West, Joe, 113
Wild Card teams/play, xxiii, 76, 132, 190
Williams, Bernie, xxiii
Williams, Ted, 88, 89, 94, 192
Wilson, Brian, xxiv
Wilson, Mookie, 152
"winning the battle of the strike zone," 182
Wins Above Replacement (WAR)
    examples/player ranking, 69–70
    meaning of, 67–68
    problems with the statistic, 70–78

Wohlers, Mark, xxiii
World Baseball Classic, 198
World Series
    1995-2018 multiple appearances, xxiii–xxiv
    Atlanta Braves, xx
    Baltimore Orioles, 7
    Boston Red Sox, xx, 74
    Chicago Cubs, 89, 148–149
    Houston Astros, xxii, 53
    Kansas City Royals, 76, 97
    New York Yankees, xx
    Oakland Athletics, 178
    Washington Nationals, 53
Wright, Jaret, xxiii

Yelich, Christian, 31, 123, 124, 171–174, 176

Zone Evaluation (ZE), 108
Zunino, Mike, 26, 80